What's FAIR got to do with it

DIVERSITY CASES FROM

ENVIRONMENTAL EDUCATORS

Edited by Tania J. Madfes

EETAP ✦ NAAEE ✦ WestEd

EDITED BY Tania J. Madfes

ISBN: 0-914409-20-4
Library of Congress Control Number: 2004107257

WestEd, a nonprofit research, development, and service agency, works with education and other communities to promote excellence, achieve equity, and improve learning for children, youth, and adults. While WestEd serves the states of Arizona, California, Nevada, and Utah as one of the nation's Regional Educational Laboratories, our agency's work extends throughout the United States and abroad. WestEd has 17 offices nationwide, from Washington and Boston to Arizona, Southern California, and headquarters in San Francisco.

For more information about WestEd, visit our Web site: WestEd.org; call 415.565.3000 or toll-free, (877) 4-WestEd; or write WestEd, 730 Harrison Street, San Francisco, CA 94107-1242.

This publication was funded by the United States Environmental Protection Agency, Office of Environmental Education, under agreement number NT-82865901-3 between the U.S. EPA and the University of Wisconsin-Stevens Point. The contents of this document do not necessarily reflect the views and policies of the United States Environmental Protection Agency or The Board of Regents of the University of Wisconsin System, nor does mention of trade names or commercial products constitute endorsement or recommendation for use.

Contents

Tables and Figures

Preface

Environmental educators are committed to increasing people's understanding of environmental issues and their ability to address those issues. It is our belief that when people are directly connected to and knowledgeable about their immediate environment, and have the necessary analytical and problem-solving skills, they will make environmentally responsible choices as individuals and groups.

For many years environmental educators have struggled to make our field — and the audiences we serve — more diverse. While we have made some progress, we still have a long way to go. We recognize that the lack of diversity is not unique to our field; however, we know we must make working with diverse populations a priority. Only through the participation of all segments of our society can we achieve a healthy and sustainable environment for all people. Working effectively with all segments of our society requires that we first examine our values and beliefs to determine why our current efforts to interact with people of color are often not as successful as we would like them to be. We need to consider how our perceptions and treatment of the environment and environmental issues either invite people in or keep them away. We need to critically examine our approaches to teaching about environmental issues to ensure that we help learners focus on underlying causes instead of symptoms. Having done all this, we will then need to make the necessary changes so that our work with diverse populations is both collaborative and equitable.

In talking with environmental education professionals it became evident that there were inadequate tools for developing the awareness and skills needed to work effectively with culturally diverse audiences and colleagues. Environmental educators need opportunities to discuss their work, reflect about issues of diversity, and develop new ways of working that will create a more inclusive field. WestEd's pioneering use of cases as a professional development tool appeared to be a means for addressing these needs. We decided to apply the case approach to our need for greater cross-cultural competency in environmental education.

Over an 18-month period, a group of dedicated and diverse professionals worked together to write cases on cultural diversity and the environment. The cases are based on the writers' real-life experiences and reflect the challenges they faced when working with cultural groups different from their own. Throughout the case development process the authors clarified their own beliefs and created a powerful tool for discussing environmental education and cultural diversity.

Each case in this collection is a candid, dramatic, highly readable first-person account of a series of events that offers a problem-based snapshot of an on-the-job dilemma. Thus the reader is offered an almost virtual experience of walking in the writer's shoes and the opportunity for analysis and self-reflection concerning a number of multicultural issues as they occur in the real world of environmental education. The cases serve as a springboard for discussing the values and issues involved in creating a more inclusive field. By capturing and using practitioner knowledge, we believe the cases will serve to better prepare environmental educators for work in and with diverse cultural communities.

Educators, administrators, and others will find that the cases are a potent tool for professional development. Many of the issues and questions raised apply to education in general and to society as a whole. The cases offer an excellent vehicle for promoting rich discussion and supporting thoughtful reflection. In a professional development setting, the cases can be used to develop strategies that can then be applied to the participants' own employment or volunteer settings.

If environmental education is to become more inclusive, it will have to change. Although change is not easy, the rewards can be profound. We hope that practitioners in the field of environmental education and beyond will use this publication as a starting point for reflection and self-transformation.

Acknowledgments

This publication was made possible through the efforts of many dedicated individuals. First and foremost we want to thank the case workshop participants. They took many risks, first in sharing their stories with each other and now with you. It took courage and honesty to talk about their uncertainty and feelings about working with diverse individuals and groups. They then worked many hours to capture their dilemmas in writing. Through a process of review, feedback, and revision the writers captured their stories in print. Dr. Tania Madfes, a senior researcher with WestEd, guided the writers through this intensive exercise. She had primary responsibility for designing the process and creating a safe environment for the writers to share their stories. Her vision kept us on track and gave us a clear sense of what was needed. Lisa LaRocque and Alma Galván, Project Del Rio codirectors, assisted with the design of the writing workshops and played a major role in pilot testing the cases.

Authors and contributors at a case development retreat. Pictured are Brady Beecham, Alvah L. Boyd, Hilda Castillo, Isabel Castillo, Elaine Jane Cole, Kathy Comisarow, Gary Cook, Alma Galván, Joe Heimlich, Hyder Hope Houston, J. Allen Johnson, Gina Lagaly, Lisa LaRocque, Tania Madfes, Augusto Medina, DouGlas Palenhus, Nick Plata, Abby Ruskey, and Dawn Wrench.

The feedback we received from pilot testing was critical to revising the cases and creating facilitator notes and discussion questions. We want to express our appreciation to Sharon Buzza at EETAP for her efficient and thoughtful handling of meeting logistics and many behind-the-scenes tasks that are too numerous to mention. We also want to thank Jim Johnson, an editor with WestEd, for his assistance in helping the writers better tell their stories while respecting what the authors needed to say.

We are pleased that the North American Association for Environmental Education (NAAEE) agreed to co-publish this book of cases along with EETAP and WestEd. As the leading professional association for environmental educators in the United States, their endorsement of the publication indicates a strong commitment to helping make the field more inclusive. NAAEE members participated in development of the cases, reviewed the manuscript, and provided helpful suggestions for improving the publication.

We want to thank WestEd for participation as the book's publisher. The agency's diverse audiences in education and human development help ensure broad access to the cases. Finally, we want to thank the U.S. Environmental Protection Agency's Office of Environmental Education. Their support of the Environmental Education and Training Partnership made it possible to undertake and complete this project.

Augusto Medina
Project Manager
Environmental Education
and Training Partnership

Abby Ruskey
President
North American Association
for Environmental Education

Introduction

When asked, "What are you taking away from this case discussion that will help you in your own work?" a discussant told us she had learned "a process for problem solving and a process to help better relate to diverse audiences." While this response may seem to attribute too much power to a single case discussion, it does represent the hoped-for impact of this collection of cases.

During the past decade, the use of cases has emerged as one of the most promising ways to reform teacher education and staff development (Sykes & Bird, 1992; J. Shulman, 1992). Staff at WestEd have been active participants in this reform effort, developing casebooks, leading case discussions, conducting seminars, and coordinating national conferences. Our experience and research affirm that theory and practice can be bridged through case discussions. Reflecting together on compelling real-life dilemmas, participants learn how to identify issues and frame problems, interpret situations from multiple perspectives, recognize crucial decision points and possibilities for action, and acknowledge potential risks and benefits inherent in any course of action.

The success of case-based work with classroom teachers, school administrators, and professional developers led us to explore with the leaders of Environmental Education and Training Partnership (EETAP) how the "case idea" could be expanded to serve those providing and managing environmental education programs. Thus the EETAP Case Initiative brought together a unique group of diverse individuals who were willing to share a disturbing incident from their own work. After discovering how the case process works, these people learned how to craft their own graphic case narratives. Working with this remarkable group has been a highlight of my professional life and I thank them for allowing me to take them on an incredible journey over an 18-month period.

The Cases

In the course of their work environmental educators interact with teachers, administrators, scientists, students, volunteers, and members of their own staff — whether they be peers, supervisors, or subordinates. It is these interactions that give rise to the kind of cultural quandaries described in this casebook. Whether the dilemmas our authors grapple with concern power relationships, conflicting ideologies, a clash of personalities, mistaken assumptions and thwarted expectations, or roles that become problematic, in every instance they are recounting real experiences that they found disturbing or otherwise challenging in their own work.

In our field tests, environmental educators across the country engaged in meaningful discussions about these cases. They explored complex, messy, and often delicate issues related to cultural diversity for which simple answers do not exist, and they found the cases to be authentic accounts of situations they could relate to and understand. In fact, at times some participants thought the case they were discussing had been written about their own organization because the incidents reminded them so vividly of situations they had actually confronted. The success of such discussions suggests that these cases might also prove useful for those outside the environmental education arena.

How to Use the Book

To complement each case, an educator who offers a unique perspective about one or more of the issues has written a short "Commentary." In addition, the special "A Comment on Culture" by Sharon Nelson-Barber provides an overarching perspective on the issues of culture and diversity that emerge throughout the collection of ten cases. These commentaries are provided as supplemental resources for those who will facilitate case discussions and as external voices for those who are reading the cases by themselves.

The chapter "Guide for the Facilitator" is designed to assist facilitators in planning for and engaging groups in meaningful discussion of the issues in these cases. Additional support is available in a "Facilitation Note" specific to each case. These notes draw upon the results of

TABLE 1. Overview of Case Issues

Case Title (Page #)	Working with youth/schools	Inter-agency collaboration	Background research & planning	Leadership skills	Power dynamics	Concepts of time	Cultural dissonance	"One size fits all"	Environmental justice
	ISSUES								
Overcoming "Biophobia"? (11)	◎		✓				◎		
Whose Time Are We Talking About? (19)	✓		✓		✓	◎	◎	✓	
To Be Expected? (27)	◎	✓	◎	✓				◎	
Perishable Partnership? (37)	◎	◎	✓	✓	◎				
Says Who? (47)			◎	✓	◎		✓		
Toxic Disinterest? (55)		✓	◎	◎	◎		◎		◎
Cultural Paralysis? (63)				◎	✓		✓		
Act Locally? (70)	✓	◎			◎				✓
Making Exceptions or Making Sense? (79)		✓				◎	◎	◎	
Welcoming Diversity? (87)	✓		✓	◎	◎		◎	✓	

KEY: ◎ = A focus of the case   ✓ = Present in the case

field test discussions at conferences and case institutes and they incorporate analyses of the issues embedded in the narrative, as well as sample discussion questions.

Many educators have written cogently about how to lead case discussions (see, for example, Barnett, Goldenstein, & Jackson, 1994; Christensen, Garvin, & Sweet, 1991; Mesa-Bains & Shulman, 1994; Silverman, Welty, & Lyon, 1992; and Wassermann, 1994, 1995). The guidance provided in this book focuses specifically on enhancing the analytic opportunities that can occur in discussion of this collection of cases. Our experience suggests that the more knowledgeable a facilitator is about the issues in a case, and the more she or he can anticipate the variety of participant responses in a case discussion, the greater the likelihood that learning will occur as a result of the discussion.

Each case provides the reader an opportunity to examine a number of issues as they occur in the real world of environmental education. Table 1 provides easy reference for locating specific issues within each case and across cases.

Because each case in this collection enables readers and discussants to examine a variety of cultural diversity issues as they occur in the real world of environmental education, we envision the cases being used to assist people in developing cultural competency. There are two major paths for doing this: one is self-reflection about one's own cultural identity and beliefs, the other involves cross-cultural experiences. Reading a case — or better yet, engaging in a facilitated discussion of a case — can lead to a better understanding of self in terms of culture as well as a better understanding of how race, ethnicity, gender, language, and power play a role in our dealings with others. Through these understandings, we hope that this resource will assist environmental educators, as well as others, in expanding their cultural knowledge and in adapting service models to better meet the needs of all populations.

Tania Madfes, Editor
WestEd, Senior Research Associate

DIVERSITY CASES FROM

Environmental
Educators

Overcoming "Biophobia"?

When applying for the job of elementary school teacher in Burundi, I visualized the environment as my strong suit, being able to use it as an integrating concept throughout my curriculum. I also hoped my skills as an informal educator would carry me through the rigors of day-to-day classroom management. I was not prepared, however, for the challenges raised by the cultural diversity in my classroom.

My fifth/sixth-grade class at the American International School was made up of students from American, European, and Anglophone African countries. Some American and European students were there because their parents worked for non-governmental agencies, embassies, and banks in East Africa, but many of the African students were enrolled because their parents wanted them to have a Western-style education in English. While my class was a mix of the urban privileged, I sensed that many of the African students were still close to their traditional values and customs, which for some included animistic religious beliefs. For many of them, this was their first experience with American-style pedagogy and curriculum. Most had a pretty good grasp of English, but in many cases it was a student's second or third language.

Over the year I became increasingly aware that most of my students, especially those from Africa, viewed the environment through a different lens than I do. Like all kids, they embraced every opportunity to get outside the classroom for such routine activities as physical education or reading under the trees. But whenever I presented real outdoor activities, I sensed trepidation. One day during recess, I happened to see a groundskeeper, with machete in hand, fussing over something. I rushed over to see what was going on and realized that he had discovered a chameleon and was about to kill it. A slew of curious kids quickly surrounded us, and before the chameleon could be harmed, I picked it up. We began to look at and talk about its independently moveable eyes, the zygodactyl feet, and the changing pigment of its skin. "But won't it hurt you?" someone clamored. "The chameleon has a place in this ecosystem," I told them, "just as all species do. We should let it go back up the tree."

I observed this sort of "biophobia" often. It came up in classroom dialogue when we were talking about the natural world, it came up when we went outside, and it came up when I presented new activities to integrate into our studies. Most of my African students had been conditioned to kill living things they found in their houses or compounds. They were taught that such things could harm them. They were also trained from a young age not to explore or play in the nearby riparian areas, forests, or fields because of snakes, crocodiles, and hippos. I understood, in theory, at least, that these learned behaviors, and the relationship to nature that they represented, helped preserve people and their culture over time. But I was convinced that by giving students positive, hands-on experiences with their natural environment, I could make a dent in their fears.

My initial approaches included planning a small schoolyard vegetable garden, setting up a compost bin, and creating a beautification project for the entrance to our school. As the year progressed, I gained more confidence in utilizing my environmental education background, so I decided to develop a themed unit that would tie into the unique area in which we lived. I presented the idea of a rainforest and primate theme to my class and they seemed very excited.

In addition to other activities, I suggested that each of my students "adopt" a chimpanzee. Throughout the prior year, I had volunteered at a chimpanzee orphanage begun by famed primatologist Jane Goodall and had gained immense satisfaction from helping to nurture many of the young orphans that poaching had created. I thought that having each student adopt a chimpanzee would help personalize the study we were doing. My own work at the orphanage had often involved helping with feedings or simply playing with the chimps, and I thought that if the students could have similar physical interaction with "their" chimpanzees, it would have a real impact on their views of the environment.

The orphanage's 15 chimpanzees, ranging from infants to sub-adults, had distinguishable facial features, Swahili or Kirundi names that often mirrored their personalities, and colorful, often sad, life histories. Like humans, each chimpanzee had unique personality traits, and I labored along with the staff to match each student with the right chimp. For example, should we match up the outspoken Ugandan girl in my class with Alley, a chimp with a similar disposition? Or would the introspective Peter be a better match?

Prior to our first visit to the orphanage, we spent several weeks immersed in math, social studies, and language arts activities relating to our rainforest and chimpanzee theme. We read about the rainforest, wrote stories, learned about chimpanzees in general as well as students' adopted chimps, and talked about the purpose of the chimpanzee orphanage. We discussed what the orphanage and setting would be like and I showed them photographs. The students worked hard and were excited about the field trip. I thought that they were well prepared for our visit. I certainly wasn't prepared for how the students reacted when they actually met the chimpanzees.

We toured the simple orphanage facilities, talked with the veterinarian about the primates' health and diet, and went over the safety rules for interacting with them. But when we actually got to the chimps, I couldn't convince the students to go near them, let alone to touch or sit down with them. For their part, the chimps stood up with outstretched arms, started showing off, and effectively begged my students to come and play. But neither their efforts nor mine could persuade any child to step up. I deemed the first field trip a near failure.

Back in the classroom, we focused on graphing the growth and weight history of the chimps, studying the reasons behind their diminishing rainforest habitat, and doing creative writing. The students still seemed interested in studying the primates.

After that first visit to the orphanage, we made a few more visits. While the kids' anxiety diminished some, those from the most traditional backgrounds continued to be fearful around the chimps.

In my efforts to give students additional environmental education opportunities, another teacher and I also formed an after-school nature club called Roots and Shoots. Jane Goodall had initiated the concept for such clubs, hoping to foster care and concern for the environment,

> I certainly wasn't prepared for how the students reacted when they actually met their "adopted" chimpanzees.

animals, and the community. We opened the club to students in third through sixth grade and supervised them in a variety of science and experiential activities, culminating in a weekend camping trip to a national park.

In the spring, on the final day of our chimpanzee-themed unit and club activities, I had arranged for Jane Goodall to visit and to watch, with parents, as my class and members of Roots and Shoots performed a play about the impacts of poaching and the importance of habitat preservation. Students also demonstrated through graphing how the health of their adopted chimpanzees had improved, and displayed their artwork. I was amazed at the level of enthusiasm and confidence they projected when they talked about their experiences. They were thrilled to meet Jane Goodall, who was celebrating 30 years of chimpanzee observation and research just down the lakeshore from us at Gombe Stream in Tanzania.

As I observed the enthusiasm and knowledge of my students, I knew I had many things to feel good about. But the students' reactions to their adopted chimpanzees continued to bother me. They never did have the experience I had envisioned for them, that of just sitting down and physically interacting with their chimpanzees. Despite other successes, I feel that I really missed some key steps in trying to counter what I continue to think of as students' "biophobia." I realize that so much more is required than just an interaction with a large, "sexy," endangered species. Reversing the learning stemming from the socialization process is difficult, but the development of a positive attitude toward one's natural surroundings is an important part of a child's education. Creating and implementing the methods best suited for attaining this objective remains a challenge. I started to wonder who learned the most from this year, the students or me?

COMMENTARY: Jane Shartzer

Overcoming "Biophobia"?

For Westerners traveling and living in Africa, it is difficult to imagine that the flora and fauna we travel thousands of miles to see could be perceived as anything but fascinating. For Africans, however, the natural world delivers sickness and mortal danger all too often. Death can result from a mosquito bite, a drink from the local stream, a small cut that becomes infected. Crocodiles routinely snatch small children; mother hippos protecting their young make quick work of river merchants; lions eat humans as readily as other meat; and mambas drop from trees, bringing swift but agonizing death to unfortunate passersby. The profusion of "exotic" grasses, flowers, shrubs, and trees that Westerners would love to transplant to their suburban gardens are scoured from African villages, which are usually barren of vegetation. There may be, perhaps, one good shade tree for community gatherings, but the rest of the village is best kept clear of plantings that could harbor dangerous insects, animals, and snakes. Because most Africans live in close proximity to nature, they are raised to guard against its very real threats.

Africans also have developed an elaborate worldview that imparts a sense of the role of humans and animals. In African stories, wise or wily animals often outsmart humans. Humans and animals are rarely partners. Depending on the culture, there is usually one animal that is regarded as very wise while humans and other animals constantly find themselves in predicaments. Africans can sense that their own precarious position is no different than that of other forms of life. Often what is taught in these stories is a healthy respect for the natural world and admiration for the traits that allow each species to survive.

Africans who leave the village and move to population centers in search of work or to continue their studies bring their village experiences with them. Maintaining ties with their village roots is important and trips "up country" to visit relatives offer opportunities to remember the survival lessons they learned growing up in their villages and impart them to their own city-raised children. Africans who go abroad for university studies, who work for multinational businesses, or who otherwise have found themselves far removed physically from their cultural roots still show vestiges of their upbringing.

It is impossible to discount the role of economics when discussing the relationship between man and nature in Africa. People are struggling to feed their families. Everything else pales in comparison. This sad fact contributes to the brutal destruction of animal habitats, the killing of endangered species, and the ravages of pollution. It is hard to explain to villagers why mountain gorilla habitats must be protected when villagers can't grow enough food for their exploding population. We decry the sale of ivory, gorilla paws, and powdered rhino horns when, in truth, the money from these sales feeds hungry children. When man must compete with animals for survival, concern for nature is lost.

The author of this case concludes, "The development of a positive attitude toward one's natural surroundings is an important part of a child's education." I believe this is a Western idea of education and not one commonly espoused in Africa. African curricula focus primarily on the three R's, taught in the dominant language of the country, rather than the local or tribal language the child may speak at home. Next in importance are life skills such as cooking, health, personal/family finances, mechanics, woodworking, sewing, and, if possible, electronics, computer technology, and secretarial skills. Education is seen as a way to escape the harshness of African experiences and to improve one's quality of life. The curriculum develops and reinforces skills that improve one's chances for success. Given this scenario, environmental studies are not regarded as a necessary part of a child's education.

In my opinion, the author's concern about the ability of isolated classroom experiences to overcome Africans' attitudes to and experiences with nature is justified. Her enthusiasm and passion for nature and her ability to plan interesting and rewarding lessons and experiences were not enough to completely change her students. I see three scenarios necessary for the kind of attitude change that she hopes for in Africa: development, eco-tourism, and education.

›› In properly developed areas, the environment no longer poses a threat to daily life. Water is safe to drink, mosquitoes don't bring malaria, and doctors can treat cuts. Dangerous animals live far enough from homes so as not to pose a threat. Daily life would not involve the need for so many precautions, and the experience and image of the environment as a threat would diminish.

›› In areas where eco-tourism has brought prosperity to the local community, there is relief from competition between man and nature. This creates an opportunity for humans to appreciate the uniqueness and beauty of their environment.

›› In local schools, the curriculum must begin to address the ideas the author promotes, beginning with the first years of education. Learning promotes appreciation, decreases fear, encourages interest, and increases understanding of the wonders of the natural world.

As these conditions evolve, Africans can gradually change their attitudes about nature and their relationship to it.

COMMENTATOR JANE SHARTZER spent the past year living in the United States while completing her doctoral degree in policy and administration at Boston University. She has worked overseas in England, Africa, and South America for almost 20 years as a teacher or administrator in private American and international schools. Her 10 years in Africa included work in Kinshasa, Zaire; Khartoum, Sudan; and Bujumbura, Burundi. In each country, Ms. Shartzer worked on local service projects addressing humanitarian or environmental issues. She traveled extensively to all parts of Africa to explore the local culture, geography, history, and wildlife. Her many visits to the mountain gorillas of Zaire and Rwanda and her volunteer work with Jane Goodall's chimpanzee orphanage in Burundi were highlights of her African experiences.

Facilitation Notes

Overcoming "Biophobia"?

An experienced informal educator from the United States takes a job as an elementary school teacher in Burundi and hopes to use the environment as an integrating concept throughout the curriculum. When she arranges for her students to "adopt" chimpanzees at a nearby chimpanzee orphanage, the students are excited but refuse to interact with the animals during their visits to the site. She is surprised by the depth of her students' fear of nature and feels compelled to help them develop a positive attitude toward their natural surroundings. This case asks people to consider how cultural myopia impacts the efforts of environmental educators who work in school settings.

What questions do we need to consider when working with diverse audiences?

In this case the author finds herself working in Africa with students from diverse backgrounds, but her situation is not much different from those in which many formal and informal educators in the United States find themselves. Classrooms and nature centers are filled with students who are recent immigrants, have limited English proficiency, and come from disparate economic strata, races, and religious groups. Even when the students appear to be homogeneous, they are not. It is important for teachers to learn about their students' personal and academic backgrounds, cultures, and learning styles so that appropriate instruction can take place. In this case, what did the teacher need to know about her students before she accused them of "biophobia" and tried to convert them to her attitudes about the environment?

How do educators respect attitudes about the environment that are different from their own and still teach stewardship?

We wonder how much the author really knew about her students and their cultures. We don't know if she ever learned whether the students reacted to the chimpanzees out of a learned fear, or because they were frightened by the sight of so many energetic animals, or simply because they were being careful in a new situation. Did the students feel safe in this unfamiliar setting? Had their fears been discussed prior to the visit? Although we know quite a bit about how the teacher prepared for the visit to the orphanage, there is much we don't know about how the students were prepared for seeing the animals.

Discussants of this case thought the author was unable to see beyond her own values and goals for the class. They felt she gave lip service to acknowledging why the students are taught to be fearful of nature, but she didn't honor their attitudes as being valid; in other words, she dismissed what was their reality. In some cultures, where survival depends upon a healthy respect for animals, there may well be more reverence for nature than we exhibit in Western society. So we need to ask, Who defines what is an appropriate attitude about the environment?

The teacher wants her students to "interact with the environment." What does this really mean? Is it necessary? Didn't the students demonstrate an understanding of the impact of poaching and the importance of habitat preservation without playing with the chimpanzees? Discussants asked whether the students could have learned to appreciate stewardship without being forced to ignore their sense of self-protection?

When is it "teaching" and when is it "advocacy"?

Although many people who discussed this case thought that the environment was a terrific way to tie subject matter together in a classroom, some were critical of how the teacher went about doing this and why. They did not think that the teacher used a constructivist approach to having the students learn about the environment. The classroom did not appear to be student-centered and instruction was not based on taking the students from where they were to where they could be in terms of knowledge and understanding. It also did not appear that the teacher scaffolded (i.e., provided small building blocks upon which new learning could develop) the experiences for her students but assumed that one thing would just lead to another. Many teachers among the discussants provided myriad suggestions for helping students learn new things, and even change old attitudes, that they thought might have been helpful in this situation.

But more than anything, discussants questioned the teacher's conviction that if the students played with the animals they would understand that their fear was unfounded. This was thought to be an imposition of values and not education.

Whose Time Are We Talking About?

It's a beautiful morning with just the hint of a front moving in. The classroom is clean and has already been blessed with the smoke of cedar. The lesson plan and all the materials are ready.

I am a biologist, working as an environmental education specialist at a national wildlife refuge in Oklahoma. This morning I will be teaching young tribal members about medicinal and edible plants.

This class, for students in the Caddo Tribe, is just one of many in the Native American Environmental Education Program that I started at this refuge during my college internship. It took a lot of work to plan, design, and finally put the program into action. My supervisor, Karen, and I came up with the idea because no such program existed in all of Oklahoma – our environmental education program was missing the participation of an entire culture. Also, many tribes, including the Apache, Caddo, Comanche, Delaware, Kiowa, and Wichita, own land that borders the refuge or is very near. How these native peoples care for their land and its wildlife can greatly affect the refuge. So we thought it essential that they be part of our program.

Being a member of the Comanche Tribe, I feel that creating this program was an honor and a privilege, a real opportunity to do something for the earth and Native Americans, not just Comanche people, but Indian people of many different tribes. When I work with students, I feel that this is an opportunity to help young Native Americans develop or strengthen their relationship with the earth, a relationship sacred to their ancestors.

While designing the program, I had a firm idea of how it would work and thought I had prepared for everything. Everything, I discovered, but one thing: "Indian time." "Indian time" is basically being late. Many of the tribes in this area run on "Indian time." If a tribe makes a reservation for 10:00 a.m., they might show up at 11:00, 11:30, or even as much as two hours late. Native American dances start on "Indian time." Folks show up at family gatherings and funerals on "Indian time." Not being from Oklahoma and having been raised away from my culture, this different perspective on time caught me by surprise.

I have asked a few elders about this concept of time and even they cannot tell me where or how it started. Some will say, "It's easy to understand, Indians are just laid-back and easygoing." I cannot accept this as an answer. I never heard that our ancestors ever practiced being late or that they were lazy. I have also been told that this way of dealing with time is a small way that Native Americans rebel against the highly structured society they have been forced to endure. It is described as a gesture against a clock-driven, industrial ethos that puts a premium on punctuality and efficiency, at the expense of the natural rhythms of life. Whatever the reason for "Indian time," it is no small problem for me because when a group shows up late, it often throws off the timing of our whole program.

For instance, the Native American class I am waiting for now is supposed to start at 9:00 a.m. I have a non-Indian class scheduled at 11:00 a.m. So if my Caddo group shows up two hours late, I'll have a big problem. Being even an hour late would overlap their instruction into the next scheduled environmental education class.

Karen and I have had many discussions concerning this problem. She tells me to try and find some way to get through to the tribal groups that are habitually late. A typical conversation on the topic goes something like this:

"Rick, isn't there some common ground or belief or principle that you can use to help them understand the importance of being here on time?"

"I've tried many ways to explain, and it just doesn't seem to make a difference. I think it may be just an excuse for being too lazy to be on time."

"Well, if they're the only class that day it may not be so bad. At least it's possible to extend the time to make sure they get a quality nature experience."

But then I worry about when a group is so late that I have to cancel their class because conducting it would interfere with another tribe's class or that of a non-Indian group. I've told Karen, "You know, if I have to cancel, it could be seen as prejudicial against Native Americans because they feel they have the right to be on "Indian time." If I make adjustments for the Indian class that impinge on a non-Indian class, like making them wait, or even cutting their time short, it also could be seen as biased, because I'm Native American."

As I look out the window, I am starting to worry whether my class will be on time this morning. It's fifteen minutes to nine and no sign of them. It's time to start praying: "Please, Creator, let them be on time!"

I have tried different strategies to encourage these groups to be prompt. I try to make their reservations as convenient for them as possible. I have told them that if they are late we will have to cut the class short, which will weaken the quality of the learning experience. I have told them, "It is important that you be here on schedule to ensure your group has plenty of time to enjoy and to learn." I have also told them, "There is another class right after yours, so it is imperative that you are here on time."

Usually their only response is to say with a little laugh, "You know how it is, Rick, we're on 'Indian time'!"

Despite it all, I think these efforts have worked to some extent. The Native American groups are not as late as they often were. And yet, they are still late for many of their programs. I would like these groups to make more of an effort to be on time, just like all the other groups that come to the refuge. I want to handle this situation carefully because I don't want them to have to race to get to the refuge. I also want to respect the beliefs and traditions of each tribe. I often wonder if I need to get more serious, or even angry, with the habitually late groups. Perhaps I need to contact people directly and get them to realize that I mean what I say about time. Then I think, Will this put too much pressure on them and possibly put the children in danger? Shouldn't it be important to the tribes to make sure that the children are here on time to learn about and build a relationship with the earth? It has crossed my mind that if I get too upset, the groups may decide not to participate in the program at all.

Where I was raised there was no excuse for being late. I was always taught to be punctual; that was important in a place like Dallas.

> **Having been raised away from my Comanche culture, this different perspective on time caught me by surprise.**

Maybe I don't understand because I was raised away from my heritage in the "big city," where everything worked by the clock. In Dallas, people would have laughed at me if I had said, "I am so sorry for being late, but you guys realize that I run on 'Indian time'!" It's very hard to be caught between two cultures and two sets of values: I can see this issue from both perspectives and I find it difficult to make it work in a way that is respectful of everyone's beliefs and norms. It causes me to be confused at times. I want to ensure that our environmental education program is reaching out to diverse cultural groups. But why is it so hard to make some tribes understand the consequences of disregarding schedules? Is it the difference between rural and urban upbringing? I go round and round — wondering if I'm just not understanding this concept of time because I was raised away from my culture, then thinking once more, Is "Indian time" really even a tradition, part of any heritage, or is it just a scam, an excuse used by people who are just too lazy to be punctual?

Wait! I hear something. It's the Caddo bus and they're exactly on time! Whew! My prayers are answered.

Whose Time Are We Talking About?

My initial reaction to Rick's case was relief: If even a Comanche is baffled by "Indian time," then perhaps I, being pale and formerly red-haired, can be forgiven for not understanding. My encounters with "Indian time" have always left me squirming on the horns of a dilemma. I don't know whether I am being culturally disrespectful by expecting to start on time or whether I and my cultural notion of punctuality are being disrespected. I still don't, but at least I'm not alone.

After my first few encounters with "Indian time," I became curious about its origins. As Rick related in his case, no one seems to know when or where this concept of time originated, but I have gathered a couple of stories.

Some claim that "Indian time" may have originated as a response to treaty-signing ceremonies. Knowing that they were going to sign away control over their way of life, tribal elders dallied. Who could blame them? Why be punctual to surrender? They decided to make the white people wait, saying through their actions, "We may not be able to control much, but we can still control when we sign. You'll have to wait." Did "Indian time" exist before these scheduled meetings with whites? In a culture without clocks, how would one know?

(Speaking of time, how is it that white culture quibbles with native peoples over minutes and hours while we make treaties to last "as long as the grass shall grow and the waters shall flow" but apparently do not know what that means?)

Others claim that "Indian time" originated in the 1960s as a reaction to the regimented and militaristic notions of time and behavior forced on native peoples in white-run boarding schools. One way native young people of the sixties could demonstrate pride and appreciation for their own culture was to rebel against white culture in general and boarding school regimentation in particular. Wristwatches, being neither native jewelry nor tools, were discarded. To be native meant to go with the natural flow, not the imposed regimentation of an artificial time ticked off second by second on a European-designed machine.

Regardless of its origins, one of the fundamental aspects of "Indian time" is respect. A colleague of mine related her experience working with tribes in Wyoming. After several months of waiting for every meeting and event to begin on "Indian time," she thought she had it figured out. So when she was invited to accompany several members of the tribe to a meeting with the elders, she decided to put her new knowledge into action. The group was scheduled to depart at 8:30 in the morning. My colleague figured this meant about 9:00 to 9:30 "Indian time," so she was in no hurry. At 8:35 she received a call from the group leader inquiring as to her whereabouts. She explained that, based on her experiences with the tribe, she thought that 8:30 meant that everyone would arrive between 9:00 and 9:30, so that's what she had planned to do. She was quickly informed, "Oh, no! We're always on time when we go to see the elders." Respect for elders, demonstrated by punctuality, trumped "Indian time" in this case.

I think my colleague's anecdote corroborates Rick's experience with the tribes in Oklahoma. As he developed relationships with the tribes over time, and earned their respect, they began to be more punctual, though still not as much as he would have liked. This seems to be a primary strategy in dealing with "Indian time": Invest your time, keep your word, and build relationships. By doing so, you earn respect, and if you are respected, "Indian time" may become less and less of a problem. My native colleagues assure me, however, that it never goes away. The only way to know if you're on "Indian time" on any particular day is to show up on time and see who else arrives.

What else can you do? Here are some additional tactics I have gathered in my conversations with others about "Indian time."

Be calm. "Indian time" will happen to you if you work with tribes. Essentially, you have two alternatives: patience or anger.

Choose patience. The worst thing you can do is to become angry and publicly criticize someone for being late. You are not a member of the community. Even Rick, a Comanche, is not a member of the Apache, Caddo, Delaware, Kiowa, or Wichita tribal communities. As he relates in his case, even he has to be careful how he handles the issue.

As much as possible, build flexibility into your schedule. As the presenter, you're the one who's going to have to adjust. In Rick's case, by scheduling his school groups so closely together, he left himself very little margin and found himself resorting to prayer as a way to solve a potential problem. He may have been praying for the best while planning for the worst.

Consider using on-time incentives. One of my friends, a Crow/Sioux, suggests, and I quote, "Food bribes are good in Indian country." For example, he suggests you advertise that donuts will be provided from 8:15 to 8:30 and that the meeting begins promptly at 8:30. Put away the donuts at 8:30 and begin. Be consistent. Cultivate a reputation for starting on time and staying on schedule. He doesn't think it will do much good, but it's worth a try.

Which brings me to my final point. My Crow/Sioux friend gave me the "on-time incentive" advice with a grin, because humor is another aspect of "Indian time." As Rick points out in his case, there's usually a little laugh that accompanies any discussion of "Indian time." I know that I've felt the joke was at my expense a few times; but I'm learning to laugh about it as well. So here's my final bit of advice: Cultivate your own "culturally sensitive" sense of humor about "Indian time." It will serve you as well as all other strategies and tactics combined.

COMMENTATOR GARY COOK is the director of Project WET USA in Bozeman, Montana. A former classroom teacher, Gary has been a professional environmental educator for over 20 years. Many of Gary's experiences with "Indian time" occurred while he was the Oklahoma Project WET coordinator.

Whose Time Are We Talking About?

An environmental education specialist at a national wildlife refuge feels he is caught between two cultures because he is a Native American who was raised in an urban environment. When dealing with habitually late Native American groups, he has little understanding of or patience with the concept of "Indian time." Ineffective communication about the importance of promptness coupled with inflexible program schedules lead to much angst for the author. The issues in this case are important for those who deliver services to diverse groups and find they must balance audience needs with program structures.

How do we deal with cultural dissonance while trying to achieve program goals?

How does Rick's own native heritage impact his dealing with the problem he presents? Does he feel compromised by making allowances for the groups or insensitive when he expects them to make more of an effort to be punctual? Where do his loyalties lie — with his native heritage or his identity as a biologist? Although discussants devoted a great deal of time to these questions, most participants identified strongly with Rick's dilemmas even though they were not Native American. The greater issue seems to be the cultural dissonance he finds when dealing with groups whose values are not the same as his own. He has developed a program to serve a particular group of people, but discussants were not sure he has a great enough understanding of the cultural norms of the group to be successful in delivering that program. Discussants wondered what type of cultural or sensitivity training might be necessary for an instructor to be successful in diverse settings, how one learns to prioritize different facets of the work to be able to balance them with the needs of the audience, and how one learns when and when not to impose one's own values.

How can our understandings of different cultural perspectives on time impact planning and implementation of a program?

A basic tenet for those who do outreach is to find out as much as possible about the clients and their needs prior to designing a program. Did Rick know about "Indian time" prior to implementing his program? Did he understand how this concept would impact the conduct of the program, or did he ignore its potential to interfere with his plans? If he had understood and accepted the notion of "Indian time," might he have built more flexibility into the scheduling of the groups? Or might he have shared with the tribes how the program would need to operate to be fiscally sound and at the same time learned what the constraints of the groups might be in regard to time. In one discussion, a participant said, "Perhaps it was the bus driver's fault and not the fault of the group at all. Did he do any inquiry about why they were late?" This led the group to consider what types of erroneous assumptions related to culture are sometimes made about the motives behind the actions of others.

One of the most interesting aspects of discussing this case was that participants reported that it is not only Native Americans who have their own concept of time. Other cultural/ethnic groups also make reference to their own ways of dealing with time (e.g., "Mexican time," "Jewish time," "Italian time"). Because "Indian time" is not the only culturally related interpretation of punctuality, participants believed that good planning should always anticipate what to do about those who are late.

How can an instructor modify a program to meet the needs of a diverse audience?

The author says he was prepared for everything except "Indian time"; but, how prepared can we really be? Put another way, how do we determine when our desire to control is out of control? The answer to both questions includes the term flexibility. If we are truly prepared, we anticipate potential problems and think about possible solutions in advance so that there is flexibility built in. If we focus on control and delivering everything in lock-step fashion, then any minor problem becomes a fiasco because there is no flexibility. Did Rick exhibit flexibility in his approaches to solving the time problem? Were his strategies effective? Did he do anything other than tell the groups why they needed to be on time? What might have been some effective strategies that would have met the needs of the groups without sacrificing the quality of the program? What if the needs of the audience had not been focused on time, but on language? How could an instructor accommodate the needs of those whose English language skills are not sufficient to fully participate in the planned activities? Discussion groups might consider the variety of needs that can arise when dealing with diverse groups and then identify the best ways to accommodate those needs.

To Be Expected?

As a non-formal educator, I was very excited about the start of another school year: I would once more be working directly with high school students and teachers through the Green Action Project (GAP). The GAP is a year-long, time-intensive program that works with high schools that include a range of socioeconomically as well as culturally and ethnically diverse students. In fact, when I started the program through our small nonprofit agency seven years ago, I designed it with diversity in mind. Yet the program had never been tried at a school quite like Hoover.

The GAP provides a framework, guidance, and resources through which a team of students develops a research-based, action-oriented environmental education project. Because its flexible structure accommodates each school's specific educational and community needs, the GAP model can be applied in any high school. As the GAP director, I spend a lot of time in the schools and in the classrooms facilitating activities, helping students gather and interpret data as they conduct research, and giving support as they plan the community outreach and service components of their projects.

This year, one urban school in particular, Hoover High School, needed extra attention and time from me. Ms. Gonzales, the GAP contact at Hoover, had agreed to run a modified version of the program. Rather than have students volunteer to participate in GAP, as an extracurricular activity, Ms. Gonzales chose to substitute this project for regular classroom assignments. She selected 17 students from her two general science classes. The group was a mix of high- and under-achieving students.

Ms. Gonzales was certain that the students would be unable to generate their own project focus, so after some initial meetings with her, I designed several project outlines as options that she then presented to the students. They chose to do a project on surface and ground water

The Green Action
Project had never
been tried at
a school quite
like Hoover.

pollution, researching the history of the city's source of drinking water and present-day pollution sources and drinking water contaminants.

Working with the students on a weekly basis, I soon came to realize that they were lacking access to resources as well as an environmental and educational base on which to build an in-depth project. They wanted to know, for example, who made sure they had clean drinking water, and when I told them that the U.S. Environmental Protection Agency (EPA) set the standards, they responded with blank stares. I was surprised because at other GAP schools, students are familiar with the EPA and most have a sufficient understanding of the agency and its role in the federal, state, and city governments. These students not only had never heard of the EPA, they were unclear about the governmental structure in general. So I spent time in the next set of visits diagramming that structure and discussing how the government interacts with and affects community issues – before I could even tell them about the EPA.

This put us slightly behind in our project plan, but the students remained interested and motivated. They looked at the national EPA water quality standards, compared them to their state's standards, and then looked at how their city measured up. Eventually they tested drinking water from various sources within the school and from a variety of sources within the city.

I became very attached to these students and really wanted to help them succeed and overcome the barriers they faced in developing their project. Ms. Gonzales and I knew that in selecting an extremely diverse group of students there would be many challenges, but we thought the benefits would be worth the extra effort. Two of the girls had little children and could not stay after school to work on the project, as many had volunteered to do. One of these girls, Renee, was extremely enthusiastic, surprising Ms. Gonzales with her dedication and involvement. Two Eastern European students barely spoke English. Yuan, the Asian American boy, stayed very quiet. Four Latino girls dominated the group. They would often talk with each other in Spanish, easily lose focus, and just giggle when they were confused.

Despite the challenges that these students had in researching a complex set of issues, interpreting the data, understanding new terms, and working as a team, they remained enthusiastic about the project. They were passionate, but very unfocused.

As our work went forward, I struggled with the attitude of the Hoover teacher. Some of her comments to me were very troublesome. She actually said to me, "I wouldn't have too high expectations for these kids." Another time she said, "I swear, they are all a bunch of morons."

All of the schools work towards the Spring GAP Conference, where each group is required to give a 20-minute presentation on their project and the issues involved. Students alternate between presenting their workshop and attending other student-led sessions. The students have a lot of room for creativity: GAP only requires that the workshops contain an oral, visual, and interactive component and an informative handout. This loose frame allows students to express themselves and convey their message in a variety of ways.

When they began their project, the Hoover students told me that their workshop would not be as good as those of the suburban students. But, they later met their peers from the other schools on several occasions, including an overnight in December when they had time to get to know one another. After the overnight, I heard comments like, "Wow, those kids are really nice," and "I didn't think we would get along so well and have so much in common." They now felt much more comfortable about presenting to others.

Although the students had really learned a lot and gained a basic understanding of a complex environmental and public health issue, they had trouble communicating it and making connections between the various components. Often I'd think, I can't tell if they get it or not. When we reviewed together, they seemed to really understand things; but when I asked them to explain to me what they learned, they couldn't. I was afraid that they couldn't pull it all together.

As the conference date approached, the Hoover students began to feel more secure about their project and presentation, but I began to worry about both. When practicing their presentation they would have their backs to the audience, read word for word in a low voice, or just tell the audience, "You can read the slide." I focused on public speaking skills and various ways to communicate to a group, but the students

When they began their project, the Hoover students told me that their workshop would not be as good as those of the suburban students.

As our work went
forward, I struggled
with the attitude of
the Hoover teacher.

did not see that they really needed to work at this and they were not committed to practicing.

A few weeks prior to the conference, I was really concerned: it was obvious that the Hoover students were less proficient compared to other schools and their presentation was inadequate. I approached Ms. Gonzales with my concerns. I told her that although the students had made much progress, they were not prepared to present alone. I suggested she facilitate the workshop to help make the connections and fill in some gaps. She was indifferent. "Oh, they'll be fine, don't worry about it," was her response to my plea on behalf of the kids. I was stuck; after all, she was their teacher.

The conference finally arrived, a fun-filled educational day. Students showed up excited to share their hard work and learn from one another. The Hoover group, in particular, seemed eager to present. I was excited too. The conference is a highlight of the GAP program and reveals much about what the students have learned. It has always been rewarding for me to see students overcome their fears, extend themselves, and leave the conference with a sense of accomplishment and pride in their hard work.

After a large group mixer, the student workshops began. I always try to catch a little of every workshop since, on some level, I work with all the schools throughout the school year. I especially wanted to see the Hoover students, hoping to witness their smiling faces and beaming eyes after they finished, knowing they had done their best in showing what they had learned in seven months.

When I peeked into the room where they were making their first presentation, I found half the kids yelling at each other. Leshaun was calling the others names. Renee was bad-mouthing the students who did not show up. Carlita and Angela were shouting at their teacher. Yuan, Emmalisa, and a few others were still trying to get through the PowerPoint presentation. Others just froze in silence when they were supposed to speak. The workshop was an absolute disaster.

The teacher announced that she refused to be in the room during the second presentation. She said, "Fine! If you guys are going to make fools of yourselves, I am not going to be part of it."

I tried to help out with a few immediate suggestions for organization and structure. Some of the students were totally defeated, while others started planning how to improve for their next session.

Their teacher basically wrote off this episode as "a disaster to be expected." I was distressed because the students told me they failed. Carlita, who had developed into a team leader, moaned, "I knew we wouldn't be able to do good." The small amount of team unity that had been created crumbled at the conference. We held several wrap-up meetings to discuss what happened. I felt that there had been some areas of success, but when we tried to understand what went wrong, it always turned into a blame session. Ms. Gonzales did not participate in these discussions, however on several occasions I heard her basically tell the kids, "You embarrassed Hoover High School and me. I don't even want to look at you."

The students now dreaded a related service project that had previously excited them and did not follow through on it. And I was concerned that this event was feeding the many stereotypes that the affluent suburban kids had in regard to urban, minority students.

When I peeked into the room where they were making their presentation, half the kids were yelling at each other. Carlita and Angela were shouting at their teacher.

COMMENTARY: Gina Lagaly

To Be Expected?

A major factor leading to the success or failure of any program is the preliminary planning leading up to its implementation. This is graphically portrayed in the case "To Be Expected?" in which both the program coordinator and the cooperating teacher appear to have left too many things to chance.

Ms. Gonzales, the lead teacher at Hoover High School, played a key role in the program's outcome. The criteria she used to identify the group of students selected for the project are not clear. Although it seemed that she wanted to develop a group with diverse ethnic origins, the young people had little other than their diversity in common. The lack of any homogeneity in the group was a detriment to their working together because they were never given the opportunity to build a cohesive team relationship that would enable them to work towards a common goal.

The GAP coordinator was well intentioned. She wanted her program to be available to even the most diverse groups of students. So when a particularly challenging group was assembled at Hoover High, she did not question whether the group could realistically be successful. She recognized that extra effort would be required of her and the group's teacher, but she thought the risk was worth taking. When students' sketchy educational background became a barrier to their success, she attempted to build their knowledge base and made numerous resources available to help them. When the Hoover students had a chance to meet and socialize with their GAP peers from neighboring schools, she was pleased for them since the experience seemed to build their confidence about what they were learning and to lessen their anxiety about making presentations to these same students later in the year. And when the time for the presentations came around, she stepped in at the last moment to teach basic presentation skills when it became apparent that the Hoover students had none. As she says, "I became very attached to these students and really wanted to help them succeed."

The GAP coordinator clearly put extra time and effort into this group and had the students' interests at heart. But how carefully did she plan for how the program would be implemented with this special group of students? What guidelines were provided to the school? Did the coordinator identify prerequisite skills and knowledge necessary for students to be successful in the GAP program, or did she assume that any and all students could be successful? Were there guidelines for how to select students, or plans for adaptations of the program for various groups? Was there consideration for limiting the program only to groups that met specific criteria? All of these questions are related to the program coordinator's planning process.

What about her relationship with Ms. Gonzales? How much did she know about Ms. Gonzales and her attitudes toward her students? How clear was the teacher's role? How clear was the role the coordinator would take? How much did the coordinator's heavy investment in the class distance Ms. Gonzales from taking more responsibility for it herself?

Programs such as GAP will work in schools. But they require careful and thoughtful planning to achieve their goals:

›› Programs will be most effective if students are selected with the idea of building a team that can work together for a common good. This kind of team building takes time, and the more challenges facing the group, the more time it takes.

›› Programs like GAP can be expected to be most successful when the students have an active role in the planning and execution of their projects.

›› Teacher-leaders in these programs must have a genuine interest in helping students find their greatest potential. This means that first they must have the belief that their students have potential. Second, they must structure experiences that challenge students to discover and use that potential. Finally, they must figure out what supports will make it possible for their students to succeed.

›› Programs that develop guidelines for implementing their models provide schools, teachers, and students with the best chance of a satisfying experience.

COMMENTATOR GINA LAGALY has spent a lifetime discovering the magic of empowering kids, especially teens. Her diverse experiences range from working with severely abused children on the psychiatric unit of an inner-city hospital to teaching science enrichment at her son's school. In 2000, she established her own foundation, Oklahoma Kids in Environmental Education, Inc. (OKIEE, Inc.). Now perched in the driver's seat of a big blue recycled school bus named Edison, she brings the magic to children across the state. High school service learners trained to conduct a variety of activities with elementary students power this unique mobile program, Eco-Motion.

Facilitation Notes

To Be Expected?

The director of an agency's outreach project with local high schools finds that the model she developed at suburban schools does not work in the same way when she tries it at an urban school. Although she devotes a great deal of time to working with students in the urban school, the results are not positive. The case presents many issues for those seeking to implement programs in a variety of settings with diverse audiences. It specifically asks the reader to assess whether the notion of "one size fits all" can or should be a workable goal and how best to determine a reasonable target audience.

Can one size fit all?

Central to this case is the expectation that a program that has proven successful in mostly suburban high school settings, where students volunteered to participate, will be just as successful in an urban high school, where students do not volunteer but are selected by the teacher to participate as part of their regular classwork. Was this a realistic expectation based upon the alignment between student skills, knowledge, and motivation and the requirements of the project? Discussants wondered how much information the author had about the students and the school context at Hoover High School before implementing the project there. Discussants also asked whether outreach programs can or should try to work in a variety of settings without examining what that would mean for the program. The author says that when she conceived the Green Action Project, she designed it with diversity in mind, but just what does this mean? Does inclusion of diverse participants — racially, ethnically, economically, geographically — carry with it responsibility for making adjustments to a model so that equity can be achieved?

In discussions of this case, many people marveled at how the case reflected the quan-

daries they themselves had encountered when trying to implement a "successful" program in diverse settings. Not one of these people, however, had stopped to examine what it was that made the program successful so that the potential for success in the new context could be evaluated and necessary adjustments could be made. Discussants agreed that knowing one's target audience is important to the efficacy of any program and that perhaps it is not wise to assume that what works with one group or in one setting will have replicable results when some of the dynamics change. Much discussion focused on the wisdom of trying to implant a fixed model/system everywhere, assuming the results would be the same.

The importance of clear expectations

The author's assumptions about the willingness of the teacher to take an active role in the project was just as erroneous as the assumption that the students would have the level of skills, knowledge, and motivation necessary to engage fully in the required activities. Discussants wondered whether there were standards and models for the school to follow in identifying participants and structuring the program or whether only loose guidelines existed. Specifically, people asked what the baseline prerequisites were for student participation (or even whether they had been specified), whether roles were specified for students, and whether students had a clear idea about what success would look like. Many found it odd that the author spent so much time at this one school and felt compelled to fill in all of the educational gaps she identified. Discussants wanted to know what the teacher was supposed to be doing. These questions led discussants to ask whether there were clear definitions for the roles of the project director and the school-site sponsor. They also wondered about how the progress of school teams was assessed and whether there was a formative evaluation process aligned with the goals of the program that could be used to provide indicators of success.

Discussants thought it important that programs working with schools provide structure and guidance for students about expectations, roles, and indicators of success. They also agreed that baseline criteria for student skills and knowledge, related to program demands, need to be developed and then applied in either a formal or informal way to help determine whether or not a program can be expected to have success with a particular group. This process would also be helpful in an early identification of what gaps might need to be filled so that all participants would have an opportunity to be successful.

What is the role of an outside agent when working with a school community?

In this case, it appears that the director of the GAP took major responsibility for directly working with the students, defining the topic for the student project, teaching presentation skills, and filling educational gaps (for example, about the structure of governmental agencies). Discussants noted that although she works with all the schools, her role in this school went far beyond what she usually does. Did she find herself spending more time in this school because she hadn't done the necessary planning that might have identified the special challenges for this group? Or, did she feel some sort of guilt about the educational inequities she found in this school? Or, did the lack of clear expectations and role definitions contribute to the teacher's limited involvement and leadership?

Because nothing is known about the background of the author or her knowledge about the learning process, we also do not know whether she had sufficient skills to facilitate learning and assess understanding as she engaged with the students. Did she simply lead students through the steps and assume they were learning? While the author indicated her desire to help these students, and to assist them with their project, discussants questioned what the students at Hoover High School really learned. Were they set up for failure because of their lack of initial investment in the problem being studied, or the way in which their involvement was structured, or even the method used to select them as participants? Discussants noted the high cost of this kind of failure if it serves to reinforce for the students and their suburban peers that they were incapable of measuring up and being successful.

So, what might have contributed to this being a more successful experience for the students? In addition to the previous suggestions, discussants thought that whenever possible, outside agents should recruit teams of teachers to work with a project. Whether the team is composed of two people, or more, the members help to support one another, provide more stability, and also contribute different skills and personalities to the activities. The team of teachers and the outside agent should then be working in a partnership to accomplish agreed-upon goals, and this takes time. Time is also an important investment when providing training or an orientation to the role of the site team; their understanding of their responsibilities and the demands of the project are critical to success. Discussants pointed out that this partnership between the outside agent and a well informed site team should be based upon good communication, trust, and a willingness to take *calculated* risks together.

Perishable Partnership?

Great, I thought, *fantastic,* when I heard River Quest's offer to enhance our environmental program with field trips and other nature activities. During our first year of helping urban youth become more familiar with their planet's web of life, we had managed to stitch together a funding patchwork of volunteers, benefactors, sponsors, and partnering agencies. Now, here was this big, influential organization offering to partner with us. What could be better than a better program? More stuff, more experiences, more resources ... yes ... and more headaches.

After only a year in operation, our non-governmental organization, A Hand Up, had a strong reputation for client service in the community, including youth tutoring sessions and after-school enrichment programs. We had pieced together a variety of resources for students from five area high schools, the majority of whom were African American and Latino.

One of our small grants provided the seed money for an environmental youth program that would grow to impact the lives of 100 culturally diverse teens. The program was structured to parallel the responsibilities and rewards of a work situation. Students were held accountable for their program responsibilities and were paid for their participation. A number of partnerships and collaborations contributed to the environmental experiences the program was able to provide. One of our partners, a nonprofit boat-building school, ran an innovative program incorporating math through carpentry. Our students were able to build two 14-foot rowboats, which we later used for collecting water samples. Another partner, a local university, gave us classroom space, and a marine biologist donated teaching time. A local car dealer provided us with a one-year, free lease on a mini-van. It was a promising start but still a nascent effort. Lacking the track record and name recognition that draws sponsors, we had major funding challenges.

It was as we were putting partners together to start our second year that I received the telephone call from River Quest, a prominent, well endowed watershed protection organization. They had received funding to administer a youth program, but they found it difficult to recruit urban youth willing to sign on to an experience that promoted only cleanup and landscaping. The enthusiasm of students who did enlist soon faded in the heat of the midday summer sun. The attrition rate was severe enough to threaten future funding. They wanted a partnership that would shift the responsibility for recruiting to us and would let them do what they do best — water-focused environmental education. Would we be interested in partnering with them to enhance our youth program? Without hesitation I agreed. I knew the two organizations had similar missions. And our organization's early experiences with partners were positive; our other partners had all been committed and supportive.

It was agreed that we would co-sponsor the youth program beginning in the spring and continuing through summer. No money was exchanged; only goods and services were to be shared. Bob, the River Quest program coordinator, and I verbally agreed to take joint responsibility for operating the program. A Hand Up would run the first half, conducting three after-school components. River Quest would conduct the last two components beginning immediately after the school year ended.

During our segment of the program, we required time and attendance sheets and emphasized punctuality. Our sessions focused on verbal and written communication skills, critical thinking, leadership development, and team building. Speakers covered such topics as environmental justice, surface transportation, land use planning, toxic waste, and air and water quality. Expectations for performance were high, not only from the adult leaders, but among student participants. The boat-building activity, for example, led to spirited competition over the acquisition of carpentry skills and the quality of the workmanship on the boats.

When River Quest's staff took over the second half of the program, the structure began to loosen. There was less formality, fewer guidelines. Safety codes were not always followed. Our secretary Debbie reported that students were allowed to arrive late and leave early without being docked pay. "What kind of message," she questioned, "does this send about employment in the real world?" Debbie also noted that students were addressing staff by their first names. And they were being allowed to choose which activities they would participate in as well as when — and whether — they would turn in assignments. If a student failed to hand in an assigned essay on the effects of water pollution on vegetation, that was okay. This new laxness was occurring in a contained classroom setting. I wondered what would happen in the field, and I soon found out.

The first field trip chaperoned by River Quest staff resulted in the suspension of a student because he walked away from the group and was missing for over 30 minutes. Was the student at fault for not following protocol? Or did he feel enabled because of the atmosphere created in the classroom?

I noticed the students struggling with the differing expectations of our two organizations and attempting to adjust. It seemed to me that loosening the standards built neither respect nor trust. What it created was an environment for manipulation and mistrust. I had not experienced anything like this with our other partners. Had I missed something in our meetings with River Quest when we designed the program and delineated our respective responsibilities and accountability?

Finally, on the five-day wilderness outing for a co-ed group of 25 young people, I had the opportunity to observe firsthand what the students were experiencing. I was appalled by the lack of structure and the number of overlooked safety procedures. Very little environmental education was taking place and then only at my prompting.

It was on the fourth day that Randall, one of the young men, got into a heated exchange with Steve, one of the River Quest staff members. Walking down the lodge hall past the kitchen doorway, Randall heard Steve call him into the kitchen. Once inside the door, he saw dishes stacked high in the sink and dirty cooking utensils cluttering the counter. Steve was clearly frustrated, but rather than enlist Randall's help to clean the kitchen, or better yet require those who had the assignment to return and finish the job, he ordered Randall to do it. Randall's response was sheer disbelief and anger. "Clean it yourself," he snapped, "or get James and Marvin to clean it." Randall's tone sparked

> Finally, on the five-day wilderness outing, I observed firsthand what the students were experiencing.

what instantly became a loud, nasty argument. From the work station separating the two, Steve picked up a kitchen knife that was lying among the dirty utensils and began to wave it in punctuation of his anger. I arrived in the doorway several steps ahead of others reacting to the commotion. Steve claimed he hadn't been aware that he was holding the knife and had no intention of using it as a weapon. Those responsible for cleaning the kitchen were called in to perform their duties. In shock, I wondered what repercussions to expect. I knew this incident would be the first topic for discussion with our partners at River Quest once I returned to my office on Monday.

On the last night, several students and I overhead a conversation between two male River Quest staff. They agreed that their own rest was more important than patrolling the corridors to keep the co-ed students in their assigned beds. They then made bets on how many of the young women would return from camp as virgins. I was outraged. Was this indicative of the value they placed on these students? Was it consistent with how they perceived their role as employees?

Over the next few weeks, I met with Bob and other senior River Quest staff to discuss how to handle the troubling incidents and how they could be prevented in the future. I thought we had worked out the difficulties, laying the groundwork for a better future between the two organizations. I felt especially hopeful because I was also asked to serve on the advisory board for another of River Quest's programs and invited to participate in a photo session with the mayor, the presidents of our two organizations, and the senior vice president of an international organization that was giving River Quest a check for a million dollars.

Surely, I thought, this "photo opportunity" signaled that our relationship with River Quest was secure and that a fair amount of future funding was guaranteed.

Wow, was that wrong. Once they received this new funding, River Quest virtually closed the door on our relationship and quit taking my telephone calls. How was I to know that A Hand Up's final appearance with River Quest would be a photo session legitimizing their work in our urban community? Well, they say a picture is worth a thousand words, they just don't say for whom.

At A Hand Up, we thought we had made the best decision about how to leverage our resources, while laying the collaborative groundwork for a long-term, culturally diverse environmental education institute. Instead we learned that, for some, inclusion comes with a price tag. This gamble to partner with River Quest rather than to go after other funding resulted in a tremendous loss to our small organization. That crumbled alliance crippled our ability to continue the program at the same level during year three. What had happened to the relationship that A Hand Up once enjoyed with this environmental education organization? Or was there ever a relationship? Were we simply funding bait, expendable in the effort to reel in the big money? How can we make sure we do not get used again?

How was I to know that our final appearance with River Quest would be a photo session legitimizing their work in our urban community?

COMMENTARY: Naomi Stein

Perishable Partnership?

What a regrettable situation! The small NGO is clearly run by a creative, resourceful, and well-intentioned staff. And, the larger organization is wisely attempting to include underserved audiences in its programming by partnering with an organization experienced in this arena. Yet, neither institution had its needs met in this failed collaboration. The small NGO did not receive its anticipated funding and River Quest can no longer leverage the NGO's access to a youth demographic to increase its reach and funding base. Furthermore, both missed an opportunity to learn valuable lessons in cultural competency that could have led to a strong partnership.

It is painful to picture the extreme incidents described in this case and to recognize the more subtle racism at play between the lines. The author's thought process in this case is completely understandable and compelling. And while we haven't heard the other side of this story, it probably would contain confusion and frustration as well.

The conflicts described provide two overlapping areas to explore. One relates to the partners' differing power, structure, mission, and experience as organizations. The other considers how gender and racial differences factored into the failure of the collaboration. Both sets of issues were compounded by the tremendous number of expectations that were left unarticulated as well as policies and procedures that were assumed rather than discussed.

It is recommended that in any collaboration, partners generate a list of questions about key approaches that should be clarified and bring them to an initial meeting. Even in discussing this case, it can be a useful exercise to generate a list of such questions. What would you ask River Quest and the NGO? What do the questions your colleagues raise tell you about their perspectives and values?

As a way to begin exploring communication and power issues in this case, you might want to establish your current level of awareness related to race and gender. What do you suppose are the race and gender of the author? What about the River Quest staff? What clues inform your conclusions?

The dynamics at play in this case indicate that the author is a woman of color and that the River Quest staff she worked with are white men. What are the telltale signs? Many different kinds of assumptions and incomplete communication can occur between people of differing gender, culture, age, and level of power.

For example, both organizations would have benefited from early conversations about how most successfully to reach their particular shared audience, how conflicts between them would be resolved, and how protocols would be communicated to staff. Such agreements should always be documented, and by being incorporated into the scope of work from the beginning, they go a long way toward promoting partners' mutual understanding and compliance.

Unstated assumptions about cultural competence got this partnership into immediate trouble. River Quest assumed either that its staff members from the dominant culture were culturally competent to work with marginalized urban youth or that cultural competence was not important. River Quest staff failed to question the NGO about the dynamics of the group being served and how the NGO had structured its program and discipline practices to meet students' perceived strengths and needs. If they had asked, they would have learned the NGO operated from the assumption that marginalized youth respond best to a very structured approach. They would have had an opportunity to explore their own assumptions that the most effective environmental education — for all students — is less formal, less structured, and more spontaneous than in typical classroom situations. By discussing these assumptions, both organizations would have been able to develop a consistent approach for working with their teenage clients and would have saved students from the dissonance that in some instances resulted in inappropriate behavior.

Further complicating this case, the youth being served were co-ed teens and environmental educators are often young themselves, with limited experience. This puts an extra burden on their employers. Long before entering the field, youth-serving organizations must draw careful boundaries for their staff, establish strategies for diffusing sexual tension, and have clear policies for particularly challenging situations, such as overnights. River Quest apparently overlooked these basic safeguards.

Finally, the author of this case wants to know, "How can we be sure we don't get used again." The NGO embraced the partnership not only to better serve clients, but also because of a hope that future funding would flow from the collaboration. When River Quest invited the author to serve on an advisory council and participate in a photo session, she assumed that this assured a continuing relationship and a new source of funding. It is quite possible, however, that River Quest provided these opportunities only to appear culturally diverse and did, in fact, "use" the NGO. Groups like River Quest that are attempting to become more multicultural have a critical responsibility to consider the depth of the commitment required to indeed become multicultural, and to recognize the dangers of one-dimensional approaches. Similarly, it is wise for NGOs to be wary of tokenism, especially of photo opportunities, as they often leverage community connections in a solely cosmetic manner.

What is perhaps the most critical and most difficult step in the partnership discussions that should take place at the beginning of a collaboration is to define expectations related to equity: What will it look like to proactively work toward goals of racial and gender equity? What will it look like when the goals are achieved?

NGOs have a responsibility to develop cultural competency and gender equity skills themselves and to ensure that all potential organizational partners share their commitment to cultural and gender equity goals. The small NGO's failure, in this case, to accurately assess River Quest's commitment to these goals caused them a tremendous loss. The NGO was approached precisely because of its track record of working well with a diverse group of youth. Especially because there was no monetary exchange, the NGO was in a good position to negotiate working terms, had they chosen to do so.

The root of much oppression is not malice but obliviousness. In all collaborations, each party must be vigilant to ensure that true respect is exchanged, and this vigilance is best manifested in regular and often difficult communication. I offer a wish to all who are engaged in the work of environmental education and the education of youth for the tenacity, clarity, and vision that it takes to truly achieve equity for all.

COMMENTATOR NAOMI STEIN has worked for 12 years at the Lawrence Hall of Science (LHS is the public science center for the University of California at Berkeley). She serves on the LHS Equity Committee and has co-authored curriculum about the use of theater for teaching problem-solving and communication skills to underserved teens. Prior to her work with LHS, she led a community-based nonprofit that served women's health needs. An avid outdoorswoman, she has led teens and children in the back country for eight years.

Facilitation Notes

Perishable Partnership?

A small non-governmental organization (NGO) in an urban setting accepts the offer to partner with a large and well endowed watershed protection agency. This partnership brought new resources to a summer environmental education program for teens that the NGO had begun the previous year; however, it also brought a change to the standards for student expectations and supervision of youth activities. When the issues are brought to the attention of the agency, the partnership ends abruptly. The author feels "victimized" and wonders how to prevent something similiar from happening again.

What drives organizational partnering decisions?

A Hand Up is a small social service NGO that provides direct services to people in the community. It has a commitment to being client-focused. The commitment to working with urban youth eventually led it to develop the environmental youth program. Many organizations and volunteers supported this program, but A Hand Up maintained the leadership — they were in control. When A Hand Up (hastily) agreed to the offer by River Quest because it meant more resources for community clients, they relinquished control of the program.

River Quest's commitment is watershed protection; involving youth was one way to enlarge the scale of its work. After receiving funding for work with teens, River Quest realized it did not have the capacity to actually recruit and directly serve them. Reaching out to an organization that had an already functioning youth program was one way to satisfy the funding agency without giving up control.

At issue here, said discussants, were two organizations whose size, scale of operations, and resources were vastly different. The consequences of a failed "partnership" were more severe for the small NGO since it did not have the manpower to cultivate other sponsors while working with River Quest. The small NGO also felt responsible for the youth and the confusion they might have experienced when the rules changed during the summer. The larger agency, because of its size, is probably used to "hits and misses," and seemed to lose nothing when the relationship ended.

How can partnering agencies share authority and responsibility when they are of different sizes and may have different goals?

At the beginning of the case the author says that the two agencies "had similar missions" and that "our other partners had all been committed and supportive." Having similar organizational missions did not necessarily mean that the goals of the two organizations would be the same in relation to the environmental education youth program. Discussants thought it possible that the actual goals and objectives for the program were not discussed in enough detail prior to the agreement to join forces. Did people at the same levels of authority share operational procedures and ways of working during an intense planning stage, or was the director

of the youth program so happy to have the additional resources for the students that she made assumptions about how things would actually happen in the summer? Discussants noted a need for joint planning and a mutual understanding about goals and ways of working if collaboration is to be successful. Somehow, the arrangement in this case did not seem to be a partnership or a collaboration; the two groups were operating separate programs with the same participants — the only thing they seemed to be sharing were the youth.

Discussants felt that one area where mutual decision-making might have prevented much conflict was the identification and hiring of staff. Discussing the details of the programs — even if they were to be operated separately — and the attributes necessary for staff would have been a useful line of inquiry. Jointly determining the screening process for selecting staff and their subsequent training might have saved the students from receiving mixed messages. In this situation we have no understanding of how or whether expectations for student and staff behavior were shared.

How do we ensure that past partnerships do not distort or bias current relationships?

At the end of the case, the author asks, "Were we simply funding bait, expendable in the effort to reel in the big money? How can we make sure we do not get used again?" Discussants empathized with her anguish and disappointment and speculated that she may not want to pursue relationships with other organizations any time soon. It is reasonable to expect that she will be wary and mistrustful of those who offer to help and her hesitancy to work with others may be justified after this experience. And yet, discussants pointed out that at the beginning of the story she accepted the offer from River Quest because all the previous partners had been committed and supportive.

So what can she do in the future that might prevent another bad episode or encourage her to take a risk? What is it that might have been learned from this failed attempt at partnering? It is these questions that discussants found most useful. They recommended that groups considering them should generate some principles of practice that will lead them to new understandings about their own working relationships.

Says Who?

It was only after receiving an email message that I realized the purpose of the grim-faced, life-size cutout figure in the lobby of my office building. Although this character with the long robe and forked spear had been lurking in the reception area for many weeks, "he" had not previously gotten my full attention. I'd dismissed him as left over from a youth event related to the "dark side" characters from some recent science fiction movie.

I work for a large state agency responsible for our physical environment. The email about the figure in the lobby was from another member of our agency's Environmental Justice Committee, clarifying the dismaying truth that this cutout character was now a *de facto* agency spokesperson.

The message revealed that this character was Torquemada, the Roman Catholic friar who had directed the entire business of the Inquisition in Spain during the 15th century. Now being featured in a campaign to discourage littering, this brutal enforcer is conservatively estimated to have been responsible for the deaths of thousands of Jews, Muslims, and other non-Catholics and the torture and displacement of untold numbers. Displaying the slogan "Litter and it will hurt," this campaign attempted to use a comic portrayal of the character's historical role to "threaten" those who stepped out of line by littering.

The message from my distressed colleague explained that this campaign idea was the brainchild of Brad, the top manager of the state program responsible for litter prevention and clean-up, and a public relations firm. The idea was based on a supposedly well-known skit by the Monty Python troupe satirizing the historical character's behavior. I hadn't seen the original skit.

The original email announcing the campaign had been sent to people in various offices associated with the internal Diversity Committee and the Environmental Justice (EJ) Committee. Both groups function in an advisory capacity for agency policymakers. I serve on the EJ Committee, whose responsibilities include outreach to minority communities.

The staff member whose message had just reached me disapproved of the campaign because of its insensitivity to the several cultural communities that had been Torquemada's victims as well as its disregard for the implications for members of Hispanic and Catholic communities: "Torquemada is a symbol of religious persecution, intimidation, humiliation, and physical torture of people. I find his choice as the agency's messenger for the new 'Litter and it will hurt' campaign to be terribly disrespectful of diversity. It offends me personally and is unjust towards humans in general."

In his email response, Brad said he didn't agree with the criticisms and felt that the lighthearted treatment of the media spots would not be in bad taste. "Because the campaign is clearly effective, I do not plan to change it. Viewing it might help you to understand the humorous context." Subsequent messages from others who had seen the campaign showed wide concern about Torquemada as a *de facto* spokesperson.

The region of the state I work in is culturally diverse and includes many Asian, Hispanic/Latino, Native American, African American, and Middle Eastern people as well as a large Jewish community. I represent about 300 staff on the EJ Committee and felt obligated to consider and respond to the issues raised by the Torquemada campaign.

My feeling was that it was simply wrong to take such a devastating part of the history of particular cultural groups and attempt to make humor out of it. It seemed to me that our agency was promoting what would be seen as an insensitive white European mindset trivializing the historical travails of the primarily Jewish and Islamic minorities of the day. But my quandary was that, despite these initially negative reactions to what I understood about the campaign, I did not want to ignore some possibility that the treatment of the topic in the TV spots could, conceivably, be so harmless as to invalidate such criticisms (that's the scientist in me).

I was also troubled about appearing to be too much of an activist. There were already doubts about the importance of the efforts being spent on environmental justice and other issues not expressly written in the laws establishing my agency's regulatory authority, and there were implications that the committee's existence was at risk. Furthermore, internal activism was not welcome: the cool, "objective" demeanor befitting scientists (unlike Einstein) was the preferred archetype ... passion wasn't.

I asked a few people whether they knew anything about the campaign and found a uniformly negative response to the TV spots. One person, unaware of the historical connections surrounding the key figure, was nonetheless critical of the tenor of the "Litter and it will hurt" message and its dark connotations. When I described the historical context, she was appalled. Meanwhile, I left a voicemail message for the sponsor of the Environmental Justice Committee, who was on vacation, briefly conveying my sense of the inappropriateness of the campaign, my attempts to keep an open mind, and my own interest in reviewing the spots for possible merit. I also expressed my surprise that the committee was not involved.

After some additional email dialogue with others who all generally agreed that the "horse was out of the barn" on this campaign – which was now concluding – and reading the explanatory message from Brad, my thoughts became clear. The message from this relatively young, white, up-and-coming professional manager explained that, while he had not been certain of the appropriateness of the campaign, he had taken steps to gain assurance by "talking with Jewish and Catholic friends" and had determined that the campaign was harmless. The impression was that he had recognized a potential problem, taken some steps he thought were right, and essentially made an executive decision that he was confident was the right one.

I was equally certain that, along with the Diversity Committee, the EJ Committee was composed of agency people with the most experience regarding issues of cultural sensitivity, and that this group should have a function other than appearing as a standing committee on some list of agency initiatives. At this point I felt confident to assert that, regardless of how well done the campaign might be, when cultural questions like these were identified, a process to seek advice from this committee should be institutionalized.

I sent the following message to the group interested in the subject: "If assurances of consultation cannot be given because EJ reps (past or present) from this agency would not be appropriate previewers/advisors

> I have been troubled by the possible career implications of pursuing my complaints.

regarding such agency outreach campaigns designed for audiences that may include potentially sensitive communities, I'd like to know why; and, why we should then continue to believe that we have genuine influence in agency activities." I felt strongly that some explanation was in order.

I received a voicemail message from the EJ committee sponsor who thanked me for my "diplomacy" and assured me of the innocuous nature of the campaigns. She would try hard to talk to me in person soon but wanted to leave the message. Several weeks went by before an accidental hallway meeting during one of my rare visits to headquarters. She apologized for having been very busy and we discussed the unchanged status of these issues. She suggested I try to view the media spots. At this point it was clear to me that the process was broken regardless of whether the spots were in fact lighthearted and entertaining to me or any other individual viewer; the facts remained that some viewers would have every right to be offended and the EJ committee had been bypassed.

All of this happened during a time frame that coincided with my taking a new position involving a whole new set of responsibilities. To complicate things, I also began working within an agency-wide team whose leader reports to Brad's domestic partner! What a "small world" my agency's managers seemed to move in.

So I have been troubled by the possible career implications of pursuing my complaints and have rationalized that this campaign is essentially over and that enough attention may already have been drawn to the issue so that a repeat seems unlikely. Despite Brad's air of confidence, maybe the attention has had the needed effect. But I'm still bothered by the long-term implications and process changes needed to clarify the role of the committee. Maybe the awful truth is that the committee is more for show than for go. Could I – should I – be ready to make this my battle? As I write, I am still mulling possible next steps. In my estimation, the privilege of the majority is the ultimate cause of such gross insensitivity.

Says Who?

In reading and discussing this case, it is the procedural or bureaucratic questions regarding who has authority to make decisions, the role of the Environmental Justice Committee, and the need for some type of review process that immediately come to mind. Another issue is the suggestion that if something is working, it is acceptable to proceed no matter how insensitive or ill conceived it might be: the end justifies the means argument. While all of these are interesting, I believe there are several more fundamental questions about change that are worth exploring in this case.

The environmental justice advisory committee described in this case exists in an advisory capacity. In other words, it advises and has no real power to initiate or require changes of departments and programs within the agency. Advisory committees can be effective if a climate of consideration and support for different ideas exists. Unfortunately, this does not appear to be the situation in this case. Instead, it seems that the environmental justice advisory committee is marginalized and was only established for appearances.

It is now the "politically correct" thing to have such committees, and their existence is enough to satisfy many that "real change" has taken place in an agency. But such a checklist mentality is typically only surface deep and does not fundamentally change how business is conducted. The result is that the real problems that brought environmental justice into existence are never dealt with in a meaningful way.

The environmental justice movement grew out of a realization by people of color that they were, as a group, disproportionately exposed to environmental pollution and toxic wastes.[1] The state and federal agencies that were supposed to address problems of environmental contamination were not doing a satisfactory job of protecting minorities from health-threatening exposure, while mainstream environmental organizations did not view "brownfield"[2] issues as a priority. As a result, people of color had to organize to bring about needed change.

But change is never easy, especially in established organizations with procedures and a chain of command. The big questions that bubble up for me in this case are about

---

[1] United Church of Christ Commission for Racial Justice. (1987). *Toxic wastes and race in the United States: A national report on the racial and socioeconomic characteristics of communities surrounding hazardous waste sites.* New York: Author.
[2] Brownfields are land areas often found in urban neighborhoods that have toxic contamination falling below levels that trigger mandatory clean-up.

why institutional change is so difficult to bring about and takes so long (the inertia of the dominant paradigm). What occurred with the anti-litter campaign is only symptomatic of a larger problem of how individuals with different ideas and viewpoints are marginalized within organizations. When these persons are a different color, ethnic background, or don't speak English well, such treatment is even more apparent. Individuals who have different ideas, raise concerns, or are not following the party line are branded troublemakers and excluded from the decision-making process. While it's easy to blame this type of behavior on the institution or bureaucracy, the reality is that such behavior takes place because of individual choices made by people like you and me within the organization. We all contribute to this condition and as a result deprive each other of potential opportunities to improve and transform our communities and ourselves.

Think about how you respond when you are confronted with new ideas or suggestions that run counter to what you believe or think. Do you listen? Do you try to understand why that person might be thinking that way? Do you ask questions that will help you understand the person's perspective? Or do you instead shut that person out? Listening and understanding do not mean that you will necessarily agree with the person's position, or that your position is any less valid or important; but at least you will have a better idea about the rationale behind the other person's thinking. With that understanding you are in a much better position to find alternatives that will work better for both of you and for the community. Until we can do this as individuals, institutions will continue marginalizing ideas and people that don't fit the dominant cultural paradigm.

COMMENTATOR DR. AUGUSTO MEDINA

has over 25 years experience in environmental education and related fields. At present he is responsible for the day-to-day operation of the Environmental Education and Training Partnership (EETAP), a consortium of 10 organizations working to increase the capacity of education professionals to deliver quality environmental education. This national project is based at the University of Wisconsin-Stevens Point and funded through the U.S. Environmental Protection Agency's Office of Environmental Education. Prior to joining EETAP, Dr. Medina was a program officer with World Wildlife Fund. He has worked with numerous government agencies and private conservation groups throughout Latin America and the Caribbean to design and implement conservation, sustainable use, and environmental education projects.

Says Who?

A state agency's new ad campaign is aimed at keeping people from littering. While the intent was humor, several people within the agency were offended because the campaign featured Torquemada, the Roman Catholic friar who directed the Spanish Inquisition. When the person responsible for the campaign was apprised of the complaints and accused of being insensitive to various cultural groups, he responded that he had checked with his friends and they felt it was fine to proceed. The agency's Environmental Justice Committee was not consulted prior to the development of this campaign and the author of the case poses some serious questions about the role of such committees.

What constitutes cultural sensitivity?

The anti-litter campaign is an example of how good intentions can go awry when there is a lack of communication and an absence of appropriate research. While the campaign was envisioned as humorous, it appears that a broad-based advisory group was not used to check out whether it would be received as intended. Personal friends of the manager who approved the campaign certainly should not have been considered "market research" for purposes of a sensitivity check since one usually has friends with similar values and viewpoints. Discussants were highly critical of the manager's chauvinistic response to the complaints brought to his attention. Another critical discussion point centered on the campaign's assumptions that a Monty Python skit represents "popular culture." Not all discussants of this case were familiar with Monty Python or the particular Torquemada parody the campaign referred to, strongly suggesting that many others in the general public would have been at least baffled if not offended by the campaign.

What is the role of advisory committees?

For people who work in large agencies or organizations, a major issue centers on the role of an advisory committee within an agency. Should they advise policymakers or offer review of policy? Must such a committee be consulted about every issue or decision in which it might have an interest? When are such committees useful and for what purposes? Are they effective in offering important perspectives on crucial issues or are they merely "window dressing" to appease critics? The author of the case poses these questions and so did case discussants. Some discussants also said that it is not unusual for diversity committees, or the people who promote diversity, to be ignored or even mocked.

What is the relationship between activism and career considerations?

Real to many people is the dilemma the author finds himself facing: should he continue to pursue the issues and risk possible repercussions or should he remain silent and hope the problems go away? Making the right decision, for the right reasons, is not always easy. Discussants tangled with questions of how to decide when to champion an unpopular point of view or challenge a decision thought to be unfair. They also addressed what factors to consider before becoming an activist or deciding to live with an injustice. These are authentic issues for discussion groups and require people to confront their personal values and biases.

Toxic Disinterest?

Reading the newspaper, I was disturbed by two letters to the editor complaining about the ignorant, irresponsible behavior of the recently immigrated Hmong people in our community: they were eating fish caught in the waters of our polluted harbor. How often our opinions are themselves ignorant! Many people didn't know or had forgotten that the Hmong were displaced from their tribal communities because they were our allies during the Vietnam War, serving as guides. After the war, the help they had provided to the United States made them targets for persecution, and many were forced to abandon their homes. As an offer of thanks and restitution, our military leaders promised them a home in the United States. Those Hmong who were relocated to our city must have been happy to find it surrounded by lakes, since living off the land and the water was second nature to them, part of their culture. Pollution was not an issue in their remote villages.

After reading the letters, I was as outraged as the authors — but for another reason. I had seen the signs proclaiming that fishing was no longer allowed due to pollution, and those signs were all in English. Did the Hmong even know the fish they caught were contaminated? It gnawed at me that they could be consuming toxic fish. I wondered why they continued to cast their lines in the harbor. Had the English-literate Hmong seen the signs and stopped fishing? Did they communicate with those who did not read English?

I knew a little about the Hmong community. As executive director of the Harbor Bay Multicultural Center, I had recently been asked by two Hmong associations to mediate an agreement that would allow them to cooperate on a single Hmong New Year celebration. The antagonisms between the Hmong Association, a group of first-generation professionals focused on delivering social services, and the United Hmong Association, those determined to keep their original cultural ways alive, are so deep that the two groups had been unable even to celebrate this

> **The signs were all in English. Did the Hmong even know the fish they caught were contaminated?**

cultural holiday together. I wondered whether these groups would have enough interaction to share information about the dangers of eating the harbor fish.

What should I do, in my role as director of the multicultural center? The center's mission includes advocating for groups whose interests have been marginalized. What responsibilities did I have in this issue? Should I investigate the facts? Initiate an advocacy campaign? I do not speak or read Hmong, but I knew I had to do something. Unless a significant number of people — Hmong as well as others — took action, those unable to read the warning signs would be at great risk. So I set up a meeting with the agency responsible for the harbor.

"What else do you want us to do?" objected Michael, the agency's assistant director. "We put signs up telling people that the chemicals in the water from the paper plants may be hazardous to their health. Isn't that enough?" I had a hard time remaining calm. "No, damn it! The signs are in English, not Hmong." Michael was unmoved. The signs never changed.

About four months later I found myself facing another issue related to what I call "toxic disinterest." It was summer, a time for fun and recreation, but I was forced to ask whether summer fun is actually accessible to everyone on an equal basis.

While Lake Michigan has miles and miles of shoreline, a number of beaches are now closed. This means no swimming. During the second week of July, the Water Environmental Federation reported in their newsletter that there were three times more beach closings in the region south of Chicago than elsewhere. This area had once dominated the world market in steel production. The price for the region's former prosperity was many polluted harbors. The affluent communities dotting Chicago's northern shores still wove water recreation into their lifestyles. But the area south of the city, a long urban stretch populated by communities of color, is where the closings were the most numerous. None of the local papers had picked up the story about this disparity. Why was it, I kept wondering, that measures were not being taken so that these beaches could stay open? Poor people already have fewer resources available to them for recreation, so a closed beach in their community, where the water is free, robs them of an important asset.

It was only by chance that I saw the story about the beach closings. I had met Rick, the federation's executive director, at a wine tasting party several months earlier. Rick must have remembered me, and sent the newsletter. So after reading it, I went to the federation offices to see what might be done to help those communities of color become more aware of what was happening to their beaches. Maybe we could create a coalition to find out why these beaches were still toxic and propose some corrective action. Who knows, maybe between the multicultural center and the federation we could make things happen. After all, wasn't there talk about environmental education groups reaching out to people of color?

Rick seemed glad to see me, gave me a nice firm handshake, and introduced me to his staff. After I shared the idea of developing a plan to make the local communities more aware of their situation and more empowered to change it, he grew quiet. To my surprise, he explained that the agency had no money for a project like this. I scanned the conference room and the federation's office suite. I saw a nonprofit organization with much dedication and few frills; this did not feel like a snow job. I felt Rick's chagrin when he went on to share the disappointing news that even after prodding by the federation's newsletter, no media outlet thought the disparity of the beach closings newsworthy. From Rick's perspective, the federation had done what it could.

Again, I felt I needed to do something. So a month later I gathered my nerve and made an appointment at the Randolph Foundation because their literature stresses the importance of supporting environmental issues. I had also discovered that the foundation was a sponsor of the Water Environmental Federation. Nancy, a program officer for the foundation, ushered me into the boardroom while sharing the names of board members whose pictures were displayed on the walls. Patiently I looked at each painting.

"These people have given a great deal to the community by creating the Randolph Foundation," Nancy stated proudly. I nodded and said, "Yes, I agree with you." I then focused the conversation on why

About four months later, I found myself facing another issue. What would have been the response if the toxic beaches were near affluent homes?

I was there. "What about working with the Harbor Bay Multicultural Center to create public awareness around the toxic beaches concentrated in communities of color? I just want you to imagine the impact of developing an action plan that empowers communities to address the problem of the toxic beaches nearest to them." I looked at Nancy. This was our first meeting. Her approval was necessary before any formal proposal could be submitted.

I sat waiting, outwardly calm but anxious inside, holding my breath. Finally her answer came. "Jim, thank you for coming to meet with me. I'm sorry to tell you that here at the Randolph Foundation we only get involved if there are policy issues at stake." That was it! No further discussion! It felt like the English signs for the Hmong all over again. Toxic disinterest.

What had I done wrong? What does it take to get a different outcome? How could toxic beaches not be a policy issue? Did some child need to die from sneaking a swim in the polluted water or eating toxic fish before a policy issue emerged? I wondered what would have been the response if the toxic beaches were near the affluent homes of Americans of European descent.

My mind flashed between the closed beaches and the Hmong predicament. Could the two issues have been brought together in some fashion? Is environmental education and action on behalf of our planet the prerogative of all its inhabitants? Maybe I should have gone to the Hmong directly and tried to put together an alliance by introducing the Hmong leaders to Rick's federation and then gone to the Randolph Foundation. Maybe I should have invited the Randolph program officer to the Harbor Bay community. Who knows, but an opportunity to build a diverse alliance had vanished.

Toxic Disinterest?

While reading this case, I found myself feeling disappointed and discouraged and also full of many questions. Here again were more examples of the "brick walls" advocates for the poor and people of color run into as they work to bring awareness, safety, and empowerment to those in our society most exposed to environmental pollution. In this story, Jim asked, "What had I done wrong?" Was his approach ineffective or were the people he approached avoiding committed action because of their social position, fear, or inability to ask questions and understand the nature of the problems?

Martin Luther King Jr. once said, "People don't get along because they fear each other. People fear each other because they don't know each other. They don't know each other because they have not properly communicated with each other." What would "proper communication" have looked like in this story?

In grappling with this question, I can't help but think about advocates working to develop support for environmental education programs in another underserved community. Comparing stories helps to analyze the issues and questions raised in "Toxic Disinterest?"

I have learned a great deal over the past two years working with environmental education stakeholders in East Oklahoma City. First, I learned how long and tedious — but worthwhile — a process it is to "communicate properly" and break down social and cultural barriers. In this African American community, Superfund* sites and landfills are located in the middle of residential neighborhoods. The residents of these neighborhoods, who had been born and raised in East Oklahoma City, took two years to identify community members, convene an organized effort, and initiate the process of education leading to change. The steps to raise awareness and engage the community in a problem-solving process started with one environmental educator who tapped into her own personal network. Connections she had made in the national environmental education community provided her with a funding source to help seed the community effort. She then convened a group of people she had known for a long time and whom she knew she could count on.

This core group included staff from the housing authority, the editor of the community newspaper, a professor of epidemiology, a third grade teacher, the director of an adult literacy program, and a legislative analyst. The environmental educator

---

*Superfund sites are hazardous waste sites identified for federal remedial action.

began by educating the group about the issues. Then this group worked to develop relationships with the city public works department, local and state elected officials, and members of the state environmental education association. From there they initiated several key activities: a training for teachers about water education issues; a series of tours of the Superfund sites for civic, business, religious, and community leaders; a series of articles about the issues in the local paper; and an environmental education exposition in the community. The group has become respected in the community for their knowledge about the issues and their access to the educational resources to address these issues. They are committed for as long as it takes to solve their neighborhood health issues, and they are attracting the interest of additional stakeholders, including potential funders.

In the case of "Toxic Disinterest?" Jim made some "cold calls" to people with influence. He did not have the benefit of a base of community support behind him that the Oklahoma team had created. I can understand why he was disappointed that his contacts failed to understand and respond when he approached them with the urgency of his concerns. There could be any number of reasons for this. From Jim's story, it appears that the disinterest was based on a lack of seeing, understanding, and appreciating the perspective he was presenting. Why was this?

In this case, all of the parties hold responsibility for "closing the social and cultural gap" that results in differential attention to environmental issues across communities. Funders, legislators, agency representatives, and heads of businesses and nonprofit organizations all hold responsibility for truly understanding the needs of their constituents and clients. They have to be willing to spend considerable time with people in the community, asking questions and listening carefully. On the other hand, advocates for those least represented in our society must be strategic, build a power base, and learn about those with whom they wish to partner.

Environmental educators working in community settings can contribute to environmental literacy and justice by working to "close the social and cultural gap." If we are committed to the goal of environmental education for all people, we must learn the tools of cultural competency and change our expectations about how quickly we will get the results we want and the way we will get them. The field of environmental education has successfully contributed to "closing the academic achievement gap" by using environmental education to enhance teaching and learning. Why not also commit to "closing the social and cultural gap," perhaps an even greater challenge to our ability to achieve environmental literacy and sustainability?

COMMENTATOR ABBY RUSKEY, codirector of the National Environmental Education Advancement Project, has spent 15 years employing environmental education as a tool to address community educational and environmental problems. Recently she has worked with community leaders in three cities as managing partner for the Demonstration Communities Project funded by the U.S. Environmental Protection Agency through the Environmental Education and Training Partnership (EETAP). She is president of the North American Association for Environmental Education.

Facilitation Notes

Toxic Disinterest?

The director of a center serving communities of color is alarmed about issues of environmental justice in his city and he feels he must take some action. In one instance, non-English-speaking Hmong are using the harbor for fishing, but the signs warning about chemical pollution are all printed in English. A few months later, he learns that pollution has caused the closing of a disproportionate number of public beaches in areas where the poorest people live, thus denying them access to what should be free recreation. He contacts people in positions of power whom he feels can help remedy the situations, but he is not successful in soliciting their cooperation. While this case is an example of good intentions going nowhere, it provides the context for discussing appropriate strategies for dealing with environmental justice issues.

How much do you need to know before jumping into action?

In each situation, Jim's first response is to contact someone of importance to help him implement his solution. He does no research and he contacts no one within either of the two impacted communities. We wonder if his well-meaning, but perhaps ill-conceived plan of action without appropriate research and coalition building stems from a widely held notion that doing the research is not considered taking an action. Is he exemplifying the "quick fix" mentality that reveres product over process? Is it possible that jumping into action can actually diminish the possibilities for future collaboration? Several discussants thought that the author's actions reflected a lack of appreciation for the difference between advocacy and activism.

Key to effectively working with diverse communities is being aware of the assumptions we make about cultures that are different from our own. Is it possible that Jim assumed that the Hmong were incapable of dealing with the problem of contaminated fish? Why didn't he make contact with the two factions of the community with whom he had some prior relationship? What prevented him from contacting the community directly to find out whether they already knew about the polluted waters but chose to disregard the warnings or, perhaps, were already dealing with the problem themselves? In the case of the closed beaches, did he know whether the population being impacted was aware of the inequities, concerned about the loss of recreational resources, or already doing something about the problem?

Productive discussion of this case has led from consideration of the following question: As an advocate for marginalized groups, what steps could Jim have taken instead of going immediately to the Water Environmental Federation or the Randolph Foundation?

What are effective strategies for involving communities in solving their own problems?

Identifying and supporting effective leaders within a community might be the first step for an advocate. Reaching out and learning about the community perceptions of issues and the priorities attached to confronting the issues should be another initial step. Before anyone can attempt to solve a problem, the problem has to be clearly identified and some importance has to be attributed to finding solutions. But for someone outside a community, what are appropriate means for initiating communication and discovering the community's concerns? Was it possible,

discussants asked, for Jim to have used the connections he already had in the various communities to do his homework, to arrange for strategic introductions, and to help educate people about the severity of the dangers that were present in the water? Might he have involved people in studying all sides of the problem and identifying potential solutions so that coalitions could have been built strategically?

Whose responsibility is it to ensure a healthy environment for all?

Most discussion participants were sure that the government has a responsibility to communicate with all segments of a community when there is a health danger. This means using every means possible to make sure that the information actually reaches all who need to know. In the case of the polluted fishing waters, participants said that if bilingual signs were not an option, then perhaps mailings to people who lived near the harbor would have been appropriate, as would notices to a variety of ethnic newspapers in the area.

A second point of agreement was that each individual has some responsibility for ensuring a healthy environment is enjoyed by all. Perhaps it was this notion that caused Jim to spring directly into action without evaluating the best way to use his energies.

Cultural Paralysis?

Much of my work over the past several years has been helping coalitions and diverse sets of individuals grapple with environmental issues facing their communities. The issues often affect an array of stakeholders with differing cultural and economic backgrounds. Recently, as a resident of one of three contiguous neighborhoods where an aging storm-water system caused chronic flooding, I was asked by a city agency to facilitate a series of meetings for various groups affected by the flooding problem. Neighborhood leaders, representatives of local business and community organizations, and officials of various government agencies were invited. These meetings were intended to focus the issues facing us, clarify the needs of the different groups, and determine a collaborative course of action.

I knew something about the groups and neighborhoods that were invited to participate, but I did not know who would actually attend. Since the collection of people being asked to work together were virtually strangers to one another, and since they would be working on a serious problem over a long period, I felt it was vital at the first session that we as a group "get to know each other." As an icebreaker, I chose a technique I've used scores of times with tremendous success. I asked people to introduce themselves and share something that they felt was unique about them. Following each person's introduction, others could react by telling whether they shared a similar characteristic or experience. In my mind, there were two purposes to this activity: to get to know each other on different levels; and to discover that things we think are unique about ourselves are sometimes shared within a group. In my experience, even this minimal amount of personal sharing helps a group build a sense of community and purpose.

Things were going great. The group of about 30 was predominately white but also included people of color and differing ethnicities. As people revealed their "uniqueness," there was laughter and good will, and I felt that overall there was a strong sense of people connecting with each other. Then a woman stood up and described a characteristic she was sure no one else in the room shared — a Native American heritage. There is a very small population of Native Americans in our city, so she felt strongly that her voice needed to be heard. She spoke proudly and eloquently about being 50 percent native and about her mother's role as a healer for a tribe descended from the ancient Hopewells. "We have a different relationship with nature than many of you," she explained. "Earth is our mother." She offered to bring that spiritual perspective to the issue of flooding in the community. "I will be the voice for the earth and native peoples," she said with quiet firmness, "to be sure our decisions are the right ones." Around the room, people were nodding their heads and murmuring agreement. I know I was.

When she finished, another woman stood and very coolly announced, "I am *75 percent* native." She was of Iroquois heritage and went on to disagree vehemently with some of the first woman's generalizations about Native Americans and the values and perceptions that she had expressed. The first woman eyed her icily.

The atmosphere in the room shifted from congeniality to tension. The air was thick with anxiety. In the wake of the exchange, people didn't know where to look or how to react. I felt paralyzed. In most situations, I could easily handle a clash of this type; but in this case, I had no understanding of the cultural "rules" that were at play. I sensed that everyone in the room had similarly "frozen." No one entered the dialogue and no one knew how to react. All I could think was that none of us understood the issue between the women and so without knowing what we would be getting involved in, none of us was willing to risk saying *anything*. The stage was set for the rest of this meeting and those that were to follow. There seemed to be a competition between the two over who was more native, a status thing having to do with bloodlines. Or perhaps the competition was more over who would speak for the larger community. The conflict was not germane to the flooding issues facing us, but there it was.

What could I have done? In retrospect, I asked myself how I might have changed the tone or feeling in the room. I wondered whether there were interventions I could have tried or tools I could have used to break the tension that first night. My style is usually very direct and I tend to state what is obvious. Why, in this case, did I freeze? What was making me so unsure of my ability to intervene?

The meetings continued. I was concerned that the tension between the two women might adversely affect the larger group. Since this was not my heritage, and the two women were from different tribes, I didn't know whether there were appropriate ways to address their conflict. I tried to talk to them individually. All I got was an acknowledgment that they did not know each other and that there were some issues between them that were not going to be solved by my trying to make things better.

Further confounding things, no one in the larger group ever publicly addressed the women's clash. Yet every week there seemed to be a sense of waiting for the confrontation. An element of negative expectation hung over the meetings. People carefully chose where to sit, to make sure they were or were not continually aligned with one woman or the other. Some participants made sure they never agreed nor disagreed directly with either of the women. There were often glances at both women before a comment was made. Aware of the continuing tension, I still felt unable to address it with the group. I was not willing to risk being culturally insensitive. My greatest hope was that someone else in the group — anyone who was not a white male — would speak out. If a person of color identified the situation we were all hostage to, the comment would not be construed as a judgment by the dominant culture. But no one ventured into the public arena with our concerns, although people of color on the committee came to me and shared their frustration over the ongoing conflict.

Despite our discomfort, the group proceeded and succeeded in developing a long-range plan. Community groups would work with their members to identify ways to reduce runoff during heavy storms and to help people change other practices that contributed to the drainage problem. The city would take immediate steps such as strategic diking of certain streets, introducing raised-bed planters, and installing water deflectors to slow water flow. In stages, over a 10-year period, the city would upgrade the major storm-overflow systems.

> The stage was set for this meeting and those that were to follow. There seemed to be a competition between the two women over who was more native.

Aware of the

continuing tension,

I still felt unable

to address it with

the group. I was not

willing to risk being

culturally insensitive.

I still wonder, however, what I could have done that might have changed the emotional tension in the room. I originally thought it was a facilitation problem, but lately I've been thinking that the issue was being afraid to treat a person of color as I would a white person. Because the women came from groups that are so minimally represented in the community, did we white members of the group amplify their voice — as if to make up for the past when they had no voice? If so, this was unfair to the larger group and to the women. They were at the meeting as equal participants. The rest of us, myself included, made them more than equal and gave them control. They did not ask for, demand, expect, or use the control; we just gave it to them.

Cultural Paralysis?

In reading the case "Cultural Paralysis?" I found myself agreeing with the author's decision to begin the first meeting with an icebreaker as a way to get everyone actively involved as well as to have people learn from one another. This technique generally produces information about each participant and demonstrates that we share a number of characteristics and common ideas.

However, after the clash between the two women, I think the author missed some opportunities to regain control of the meetings. For example, if he had reemphasized the purpose of the meetings and recognized the positive aspects of the diverse group, the differences between the two women's representation of Native American culture might have been viewed more positively. He might also have begun every succeeding meeting with an icebreaker intended to lighten the atmosphere.

Another strategy would have been to do some advanced research prior to the first meeting in order to become familiar with potential participants and community dynamics. This would have helped prepare him for any potential surprises and would have equipped him with background information on relevant cultural differences as well as cultural etiquette to help him perform the assigned tasks more effectively.

By not addressing the tension between the two women and just moving forward with the meetings, I'm not sure the group delivered its best work or developed the best plan. However, it is important to note the bottom line: the group was able to carry on and a plan was completed despite the distraction caused by the conflict between the two women.

When I was in a similar situation with a diverse group of business people, elected officials, community residents, and representatives of faith-based organizations — all from different cultural and economic backgrounds — I used an icebreaker at each session. At one meeting I asked participants to look at the person on their left and tell that person three positive things they had learned about him or her since the first meeting. After that exercise, I turned to one of the individuals who was creating negative tension in the group and asked him to be the facilitator for the meeting. Consequently, he had to focus on the issues and keep the meeting going with the provided agenda. This strategy worked so well that at a subsequent meeting I drafted another person to facilitate the meeting, and again it worked with great success.

The most important thing I did at every meeting, however, was to state our purpose and ask everyone to think about how they could be part of the solution rather than part of the problem. I also asked the participants to remember that everyone has something to contribute, so respect for each other's points of view was very important.

This case gives the reader much to think about. I experienced it as an invitation for those of us in the environmental education arena to assess our techniques. As we expand our contributions to the field, our ability to stay focused while navigating sometimes difficult group dynamics will become increasingly important.

COMMENTATOR ALVAH BOYD is presently CEO and president of the Northeast Homeownership Consortium, Inc. in Oklahoma City. She is also vice chair of the Oklahoma City Housing Authority Board of Commissioners, vice chair of the Metro Area Development Corporation (a Small Business Administration 504 Loan Program), a member of Oklahoma City's Empowerment Zone/Enterprise Community Governance Committee, as well as chair of the Oklahoma City Empowerment Zone/Enterprise Community Education Committee.

Facilitation Notes

Cultural Paralysis?

An experienced facilitator is asked by a city agency to chair a series of community meetings. These meetings are to help determine a collaborative course of action to be taken after flooding occurred in several neighborhoods. A serious dispute between two participants, which erupts at the beginning of the first meeting, creates tension in the group for the remainder of the meetings. The facilitator feels incapable of interceding because he doesn't understand the cultural "rules" at play and none of the other participants wants to risk offending either of the women. Is this a case about facilitation skill or cultural understandings?

How does the facilitator create an environment of equality, trust, and respect?

The easier issues to discuss are related to facilitation and the role of a facilitator: What are effective ways to help "break the ice" when beginning to work with a new group of people? Was the choice of the icebreaker used in this case appropriate for the group? How important is it to form community among strangers who must work together? How does one prepare for a multicultural meeting?

Those who often chair meetings have little difficulty responding to these questions and offering advice or opinions about the best ways to start meetings. There is much agreement about the importance of developing a shared sense of purpose within a group. While the techniques used in facilitation are easily discussed, the critique of the author as a skilled facilitator does not come easily. Some discussants questioned whether he possessed the skills necessary for dealing with diverse groups and whether he adequately anticipated the variety of problems that might arise when disparate individuals are asked to work together in a voluntary fashion. An important question to pose to the discussants is How do you create a cultural norm for a diverse group?

What is the role of the facilitator (and/or group member) when there is tension between members of a group?

In this case, neither the facilitator nor any group member took action to help minimize the palpable tension in the group caused by the conflict between the two women. What could the facilitator have done to increase the comfort level of the group? What could he have done to minimize the conflict between the two women? How did the group empower the two women to continue their feud? Discussants were able to answer these questions related to the specifics of the case quite easily. But more important are the same questions framed in a more general way: Should a facilitator (or group member) always intercede when there is tension between members of a group? How should a facilitator (or group member) intercede when

the tension impacts the group's working atmosphere? What is the role of group members in ensuring successful outcomes? These more general questions require definitions of personal responsibility and acknowledgment of required risk-taking behaviors.

How does race impact the ways in which we relate to people?

Although the author says that the conflict between the two women is over who is "more native," or has the right to represent things native, discussants wondered whether the author had made an assumption about the homogeneity of Native American culture. We have to ask ourselves about our preconceived notions of homogeneity within various cultural groups and whether this is a form of stereotyping that interferes with our ability to relate to people as individuals. Is it this preconception about different cultural groups that has created the "cultural paralysis" in the title of the case? Did the author feel powerless because he feared offending the women who were from a small minority group; did his fear override his use of common sense? Did culture and ethnicity play a bigger role than they should have in the proceedings of the group? Did the author's sensitivity to bearing "the white man's guilt" prevent him from being assertive in his role as facilitator? These are the difficult questions that can and should be addressed during the discussion.

Act Locally?

I'm a firm proponent of *act locally, think globally*, a view that has made me feel misunderstood by many of my colleagues. Some of the national environmental groups, seeing me as territorial and unapproachable, may have thought I have a bad attitude about working together. But as I explained to my close friend and co-worker from Mexico, what I really have is a different philosophical view of what it means to "work with" others on environmental education. During the past 13 years, working along the United States/Mexico border as a community organizer on environmental and health water issues, I've been dismayed at the havoc national economic interests can play with the lives of local people. I'm only interested in partners who are serious about improving those lives.

Over 20 years ago the United States forced Mexico's hand in paying back its international trade debt. Mexico's strategy was to establish the *maquiladora* program: stringing foreign-owned assembly plants along her side of the border to take advantage of cheap labor, understaffed regulatory agencies, and exemptions from municipal taxes that might otherwise pay for infrastructure. What it created besides jobs was a burgeoning population without the funds, political power, or collective voice to do anything about their hazardous living conditions. Today thousands of people still live in shantytowns where poor water and sanitation cause dysentery, hepatitis A, cholera, and tuberculosis at levels up to three times the U.S. national average. Given that the environment knows no political boundaries, both sides of the border have many social and environmental problems to address.

When the North American Free Trade Agreement was being promoted, the media exposed and even sensationalized the border's problems, leaving residents angry, confused, and frustrated. Lots of federal money was initially invested to show the government's good intentions, but it was not enough to undo decades of callous neglect. How did this environmental degradation build up to such a serious level? Why had residents received so few benefits from the industrial development? And how could they improve conditions when the drive for the economy and trade accelerated at a faster pace than the communities could mobilize?

Because of the critical need to build community capacity along the border, my Mexican co-worker and I have taken our charge very seriously. Our focus is intense — working with 50 U.S. and Mexican teachers over many years to develop students' critical-thinking and problem-solving skills in the context of real-world investigations. Students look at the impacts of raw sewage in the river, health problems related to a lack of potable water, and riparian and wildlife habitat destruction of an area managed for floods and illegal immigrants. It's been a long haul examining various teaching practices, building student competencies, and strengthening local networks. We have learned so much through trial and error about what it takes, both culturally and educationally, to help empower communities to bring about change.

Over the years, we have established solid networks with public health, agricultural, urban, and ecological organizations. Several former students are now in the communities serving as resources. Six of the original 10 teachers have been with the program for all 13 years. Agencies, community groups, and schools have respected our balanced approach and often agreed to engage in tough discussions of equity and environmental dilemmas in order to move the dialog among stakeholders forward. We are known for our high standards and investment in the community. But despite our good reputation, our funding has always been hand-to-mouth.

We feel a real sense of urgency and commitment to our communities. We cringe when we see money spent for superficial educational activities, such as models recreating the water cycle, or for only cursory attention to skills border students need now, such as learning how to respond to the immediate environmental challenges we face. Lots of programs have come and gone, abandoning plans or leaving reports on the shelf. I don't understand how they can come into the communities and not see the urgent challenges we face. Or, perhaps, see and do nothing.

Two years ago, Tech Ecology, a newly formed organization, got a multimillion-dollar grant to combine technology and environmental

Despite our good reputation, our funding has always been hand-to-mouth.

monitoring. I found out about it the day before they submitted their proposal. I was out of town, in the middle of running a three-day workshop, when my office called to tell me about an urgent message from someone at a university outside our region. It turned out to be Jack Strong, the director of this new organization.

I left during a break to call him. Without much introduction or inquiry about our program, Jack said, "I've heard great things about your program and want you to write a letter of support saying that you would help us connect your schools to our program." I broke in and replied, "We haven't been able to devote much to technology because there have been so many obstacles in getting computers up and running in the schools, but we have made great strides in educational reform practices that seem to really push critical thinking." Jack quickly dismissed me, "The program is set. We have lots of big names behind it from the university. The letter is all I need — you know how crazy it is to put these big proposals together. Is there any chance you could get it to us today?"

The proposal was due in 24 hours and I already knew that the request for proposals had a requirement to include minorities — that is where our region fit in. His university was 300 miles away. I was a little frazzled from being pulled away from our workshop and had to tell him that given the rushed schedule and limited opportunity to talk I just couldn't help him out.

Months later, Sandy, one of my teachers, called and said, "I just wanted to call so you heard it from me firsthand. I have been approached by Tech Ecology and they are offering our school $50,000 worth of equipment. Their program is similar to yours, but not with the same level of educational depth and experience. I just can't turn down the equipment. It's the only way our school could ever get it. Although, honestly, I still don't know who can set it up, maintain it, or fix it. Let's hope that Tech Ecology does. They haven't been able to answer my questions yet. But I just wanted to let you know that I'm not dropping out of your program either. I have gotten so much out of it." Later five other teachers let me know they too were involved with Tech Ecology; only one dropped out of our program, saying he was already juggling too much.

It was interesting to see that the same dedicated teachers pursued the opportunities whether they involved modest financial support (as in my program) or a "golden carrot" of technology. I have to admit to a great deal of pride in "my teachers." Given the challenges of working in border schools, with their lack of resources, dwindling budgets, increasingly narrow focus on accountability, high staff turnover, and backdrop of unrelieved societal problems, most teachers struggle simply to survive. Those with the energy to work toward change are few, and precious. How could I begrudge them the equipment? But at the same time, I saw no real value in trying to combine our efforts with organizations like Tech Ecology that didn't even look our way (or at any local entities) during the planning and implementation process. Jack had been quite clear that he just wanted the letter.

Except for bits of gossip from my teachers about how Tech Ecology mentioned us as a group with whom they were working, I never heard from them. The teachers' concerns about technology proved well founded. It took them almost eight months to find someone to set things up, and they're still struggling with technological glitches.

This year, I got another call from Jack Strong. He said that he had written $5,000 into this year's budget to put some curriculum on their Web site. Did we want to write it? I could see that his sense of "working together" hadn't changed much. Our work was about innovative teaching practices and learning processes, not about packaged curriculum. I tried to explain this to Jack, but he didn't seem to be listening. I suggested he speak with Sandy or come to a workshop, but I never saw any evidence of his interest. So in the end, I said no. Given his actions it just didn't seem worth the effort.

I was upset by this token offer that had taken two years to surface. The work we developed had been tested for 13 years and this gesture didn't represent the recognition I felt our program deserved. He'd already seen firsthand how successful our teachers had been in Tech Ecology's program. We were there for the long haul, forming deep relationships with the community because we were all members of it. The dominant American culture promotes competition, domination of resources, and a sense of individual efficacy over interrelationships. My

I was upset by the token offer from Tech Ecology. This gesture didn't represent the recognition I felt our program deserved.

I realized there might be repercussions for our project's reputation, but I had to say no.

life in this community demands another set of values. This was not the first time a national group wanted free "how-to" information or access to the populations we serve so they could meet their funding requirements. But our work is not about meeting demographic quotas, it's about partnering with members of a community to improve the quality of their environment and their lives. I realized that there might be repercussions for our project's reputation, but I had to say no.

Act Locally?

As I read this case many complex questions came to mind. What is it that really drives an organization to develop projects? And in turn, what really motivates donors to provide funding? Is it that they want to support society's status quo or do they really want to bring about meaningful change? How is it decided who develops the projects and whether a project is really needed by the communities for which it is designed?

This case clearly demonstrates the disparate power relationships that exist among individuals at the community, regional, and national levels, whether in education, the environment, or other areas. It highlights the injustice that many small organizations suffer as they respond to the challenges of globalization while still struggling to achieve their objectives within the community. The current approach to project development and funding leaves out an important group of people who historically have been disenfranchised and for whom few have time (because working with them is time-consuming and requires different processes from those that funding groups typically support). The prevalence of large organizations obtaining funding for local projects often negates the value and strength of community relationships, once the foundation of our society and still a fundamental tenet of Latino culture.

This case exemplifies the waste of resources that result when organizations try to work at the local level without the participation of local groups and community members. Tech Ecology's budget is huge compared to that of the author's community-based organization. Clearly, Tech Ecology does not have the energy, time, or experience to undertake the grassroots work needed to ensure the long-term success of the program. At the same time, the local group does not have the facilities, equipment, and expertise necessary to manage the large-scale project that the donor wants to support. If it would try to compete with the larger group, which has greater access to technology, management of information, resources, and power, it would have to do so at the expense of the community work it is committed to doing. And if it was successful in attracting the funding, how could the small group sustain a large budget in an area that does not have the infrastructure to support it?

Is the only answer for small organizations to remain silent and follow the path or directives of national projects that may meet broad goals but seldom are rooted in the community, and therefore do not effectively address local needs? How does a small local organization resolve the dilemma of trying to meet funders' requirements that may not address the real needs of the community? Does it mean that small community groups must show one face to the funding organization while showing a totally different face to the community?

Do *inclusiveness* and *teamwork* apply only at the local level and not at the national level? If so, whose responsibility is it to inform members of the dominant culture about how to function at the local level? Are the historical patterns of conquering indigenous groups or the neocolonialism that continues to shape the economies of developing countries operating here in a more subtle way?

What is the message embedded in this prevalent pattern of the large group getting to dictate what and how the work will be done, who will do the work, and how the resources will be spent? Is it that solutions to local problems do not require that the affected people be involved in the process? Is there another message that technology can fix any problem, even though the fundamental characteristics of the community and local knowledge are ignored instead of used as the starting point? These persistent messages demand that we stop and examine our real priorities.

These overarching issues are crystallized for us in this case in a rather personal way, when the author receives a last-minute request for a letter – the day before the grant application is due – from a large organization. Deeming this a token offer driven by the requirement to include minorities, she faces the dilemma of choosing between potential funding or maintaining a sense of program integrity.

The local group has worked long and hard to build a program focused precisely on the critical thinking and problem solving needed to address health problems and reverse environmental degradation. The fact that Jack Strong displayed scant knowledge of or interest in the substance of the program, known for its high standards and commitment to the community, suggests to the author that this is another national group wanting free "how-to" information or access to diverse populations with little if any acknowledgment of or role for a group that has spent years developing relationships and the trust of community members.

At the same time, I wonder about the author's underlying rationale for rejecting Tech Ecology's request so quickly, especially when she didn't know the details of the proposal. In this case the small organization assumed that Tech Ecology was not at all interested in processes. However, two years later they returned with another offer, which might have been more inclusive if a relationship had been nurtured. What might have happened if the initial offer had been accepted and it was used to start a dialogue with Tech Ecology about the value of another approach? Might the second offer have been better, or would it have been made at all? Is it necessary to have a hidden agenda in order to achieve one's objectives?

This commentary has raised more questions than it answered. Fundamentally it is seeking more affirmative and constructive ways for local, regional, and national organizations to work together to address community needs. But ultimately it is about how we as a society value and respect what each of us has to offer. Everyone of us has the right to self-determination and the obligation to accept the consequences of our decisions.

COMMENTATOR ALMA GALVÁN has a degree in educational psychology and is working towards her MA in public health. She has 17 years experience in the design, implementation, and assessment of binational programs in environmental education, public health, and community organizing. She is from the northern border state of Chihuahua, Mexico.

Facilitation Notes

Act Locally?

When contacted at the last moment by an organization requesting a letter of support for a funding proposal, the author of this case says no. As a community organizer who has long worked along the United States/Mexico border on environmental and health water issues, she is offended when outsiders don't take the time to find out what the needs of the community really are, and she feels slighted when her work is not recognized. A major question confronted through discussion of this case is What obligations do organizations have to support each other's efforts?

What is at stake for the author, the participating teachers, and Tech Ecology?

Discussants recognized that there is an emotional undercurrent in this story. The author seems to be angry that others don't recognize all she has done for the community

over such a long period of time with limited resources. She refers to the teachers as "my teachers" and sees herself as the gatekeeper for providing access to them. Is it possible she feels vulnerable to being pushed aside by bigger, wealthier change agents? What is at stake that makes her so determined to be uncooperative when the schools would benefit? Did she not consider ways in which this could have been a win/win situation? When she decides that there is "no real value in trying to combine our efforts with organizations like Tech Ecology," how does this impact the teachers? Do they find themselves caught in the middle between competing forces — one with a history of good work and the other with the promise of sought-after technology? If Tech Ecology is geographically distant from the border community, does the loss of a local collaborator damage its ability to accomplish the goals of the project? Why wasn't the time taken to cultivate the author prior to requesting her help? Was it arrogance or ignorance that resulted in not building important relationships and learning what would be most beneficial to all concerned? Has Tech Ecology set itself up for possible failure because the local people could actually sabotage their efforts?

What differences exist between local and national groups that hinder closer collaboration? How might these be overcome?

This case exemplifies how the failure to establish relationships between two groups with complementary expertise results in the loss of opportunities all around. Lively group discussions have taken place when participants represented both small local organizations and large national entities: they all recognized the forces at play within this case. Discussants said small local groups are usually more flexible than the larger organizations, whose rigid bureaucracies dictate policies and procedures – often prescribing formulas for engaging with local communities. While the smaller groups have limited resources and staff, they are often better at relating to local communities because they are of the community, whereas the outside organizations have a difficult time understanding the local environment. After identifying the differences between local and national groups, discussants have suggested steps to be taken by both sides if they want to have better relationships.

Who determines local needs?

While reading the case, it is hard not to wonder whether the author could have worked at persuading Tech Ecology to see and do the right things for the local population. But what are the "right things"? Who determines what the local needs are and how they should be satisfied – the community or the activists? How could the author have gone about turning this into a situation that would have benefited everyone?

What obligations do organizations have to support each other's work?

Although the author seems to be quite territorial about the teachers and schools on the border, she is justified in feeling insulted by the last-minute requests for help and support. People do not like to feel that they or their accomplishments are being disrespected or that their time is not worthy of consideration. So after acknowledging the very real emotions at play here, discussants moved to a more general question about organizational responsibility. If the same clients are involved with more than one group, how much support can they expect from those who interact with them? What are the benefits and disadvantages of partnerships and collaborations? How can small local groups better leverage the assets of bigger organizations? And how can large organizations better utilize the know-how of small local groups without rolling over them in the process?

Making Exceptions or Making Sense?

The day Groundwater Guardian registration closed, I checked the mail and recounted envelopes – 50 communities had renewed and seven new communities had signed on. But the application I most wanted to see, from a northwestern Native American community, was nowhere to be found. I hoped it was just a late postmark. On Friday, the postmark theory discarded, I called the reservation.

Groundwater Guardian is based on one of the great strengths of environmental protection: to paraphrase the old political line, it's all local. Citizen leaders in small communities set priorities, marshal local support, and save groundwater community by community. In return, we connect these communities to the latest government research, celebrate their efforts, and help to facilitate their programs. Over 15 years, Groundwater Guardian has expanded from a few scattered communities to a centerpiece of our parent foundation's work.

I had recently joined the program staff as a fresh college graduate with more enthusiasm than experience. My biology degree emphasized lab technique over people skills, but I was excited to apply my scientific knowledge on a grassroots level. The year I joined, the program was busy expanding to eight new sites spread around the country, linked by the need to protect their drinking water supply and a willingness to participate in the program. Being new myself, I felt a special connection to these new communities.

The team I was so eager to hear from was our foundation's first attempt to involve a tribal community in Groundwater Guardian. Although the foundation had worked nationally to identify groundwater threats on reservations, we had not previously tried to engage a tribal community at this level. We approached this tribe, which was recommended to us by a national partner, because the cleanliness of the tribe's main source of drinking water was threatened by industrial development. Tribal members were supportive of the program and enthusiastic about participating.

The team I was so eager to hear from was our foundation's first attempt to involve a tribal community in Groundwater Guardian.

From the beginning, however, there had been challenges. The first step in the program is setting up a governing team, usually composed of local citizens and volunteers. On the reservation, while enthusiasm remained high, individuals seemed to resist participation. "Talk to the elders," we were told again and again. For an organization that prizes grassroots action, this was a real conundrum. We were interested in local citizens acting voluntarily on behalf of the water, but no matter how many times we explained the grassroots nature of the program, no matter how much interest we elicited, the listener always suggested we confer with the tribal elders. Instead of citizen volunteers, the tribe seemed determined to choose the very same top-down decision structure the program was designed to counteract – the buck didn't seem to stop anywhere but with the elders of the tribe.

In the end, a compromise was struck: local citizens and tribal officials would cooperate on the Guardian team and the elders would give tacit approval to its plans. Although certainly looking different than the other community teams, the staff had decided that the underlying principles were local control and citizen participation – if those local citizens happened to be the tribal heads, then so be it.

In the course of these discussions my boss had traveled to the reservation to meet with the team personally and talk with the elders, and, once hired, I spent countless hours on the phone with them. In fact, our long distance bill to the reservation and the time we spent getting their cooperation dwarfed that for any other community. Perhaps because of the rapport that we seemed to have developed, I was especially surprised when, on deadline day, neither their application form nor an explanation appeared. When I called the reservation and spoke with the team leader, she was as gracious as ever and not a bit surprised that I didn't have their application. "It's here on my desk," she told me. "I'll get to it soon."

I hung up, stunned by the contrast between her nonchalance and my palpable anxiety. I mentally reviewed general lessons about cultural differences of time and the importance of paperwork, but that didn't change the fact that I needed her application form. Our deadline wasn't arbitrary, it was set by our grant requirements, and I needed the information in the application to start setting up our part of the program. For one thing, that information justified continued funding. We are supported almost entirely on grant money and it's important to demonstrate to funders that communities are participating fully — something we gauge from the information they give us on these forms. A group that repeatedly drops the ball on paperwork may lack the necessary follow-through. Morever, we are best able to provide support for a community when we know what they are up to. If we don't get their forms, we are less able to advise them.

That night, I thought back over what seemed like my constant communication with the team leader. Had I not been entirely clear on the timetable and expectations for participation? Had I misread their enthusiasm about the program? Were we pushing Groundwater Guardian without tribal support? And on a practical level, what about new deadlines?

The following Tuesday, the team leader assured me that the team was working on their paperwork and that I'd have it within the week. I calmed down when my boss said that there was flexibility in our timetable. The form arrived the following week and went on to our funders with no repercussions.

The tribe celebrated becoming a GG community with a Salmon River parade. The team continued in the program for three years — but with little improvement in promptness. We wrestled with always changing our boundaries to accommodate this partnership. We felt our program had reasonable expectations, clear guidelines, and lots of support for communities, so it seemed little to ask that communities turn in their forms on time. Being constantly put in a position of changing the rules for the tribe made us question the fairness of the rules. How could we claim to be running a fair program if the standards for participation changed for each community? In our organization, we try to apply the same high standards to everyone because we believe that groundwater protection requires the best of each of us. So we looked, and are still looking, for ways to avoid patronizing tribes with deadline extensions and reminder phone calls, to maintain the integrity of our program, and to still include them. It didn't help that the non-tribal communities were meeting program expectations with no problem at all.

Perhaps because of the rapport that we seemed to have developed, I was especially surprised when, on deadline day, neither an application form nor an explanation appeared.

Working with this tribe helped us see the assumptions we were making about who our audience was. Our program was for the white, middle class of America. We suggested that teams work with their city council, communicate with us by fax or email, and use a bottom-up organization for best results. Our guidelines demanded that certain paperwork be completed and that results be documented. Because these suggestions and guidelines had worked well before, we were ignorant of how a culture different from that of our other teams might respond to them. We don't know yet how to generalize the lessons from this experience — especially given the variations among and within cultural groups. But we recognize that we have come upon the perhaps inevitable dissonance of requiring quantitative results from a community that considers itself inherently qualitative.

At the end of their third year, the tribe dropped out. I've talked with the team leader about renewing their participation, but she tells me that although there is interest in protecting groundwater, their priorities have changed.

There are now 161 Groundwater Guardian communities and not one is a tribal community.

Making Exceptions or Making Sense?

It is important for those who are working with Indian tribal or Indian educational organizations to be aware of cultural differences between native peoples and the dominant society. In reviewing this case, the main difference seems to be around concepts of time. The tribal organization in question did not complete, on time, the Groundwater Guardian application and thus demonstrate their willingness to participate in the program.

Usually tribal volunteers making a decision that would impact the entire tribe have to obtain approval from the elders of the tribe. The elders of most tribal governments — especially those on most reservations in this country — normally provide the final approval. In many cases, it may take elders several days or even weeks before a decision is made because their deliberations are based upon tribal traditions that have been passed down through generations. Time is not an element to consider when a decision about a commitment of the entire tribe is given to the elders.

Tension and conflict about time between those from the dominant culture and native peoples usually produce references to "Indian time." "Indian time" has several definitions depending upon the Indian person with whom you are speaking, his or her tribe, and whether the person is from an urban, rural, or reservation location within the United States or Canada. But the most common applications of the concept are found when Indian people are late and say they are running on "Indian time" or when Indian people wait until the last minute, or whenever they feel it necessary, to complete a task and say they are on "Indian time." I have had colleagues who waited until the last minute to complete major grant applications that had specific deadline dates and then submitted them late. As a result, many students lost tutorial assistance and valuable scholarships. In some cases the person was fired for such behaviors.

I knew that during the early years many Indian people, especially the elders, did not own a watch or a clock and felt these were devices used to control by the dominant society. They had little use for the "white man's time," especially on the reservation. Several years ago I surveyed tribal elders from a number of Indian tribes throughout the western part of the United States to find out their definition of "Indian time." Some of their responses follow:

>> The dominant society values time, the traditional Indian does not.

›› Time is money and we have very little.

›› How do you waste time when you don't have a watch?

›› How do you save time when the clock never stops?

›› Why is time so important to the dominant society?

›› Why is time more important than people?

›› Why are most people controlled by a clock?

In all Indian traditional cultures, respect for our elders is much more important than respect for time or money. As one of the elders stated in his survey response, "Respect for people wins over the respect for a machine such as a watch or a clock." All of the elders concurred that "Indian time" is when Indian people are ready to go somewhere or do something on their own time.

Being Native American, raised and educated in the state of Oklahoma, and having worked in the field of Indian education for the past 28 years, I have experienced various models of "Indian time." First of all, we had to be at school and church on time, with no exceptions. The parents and grandparents of Indian children always set the time or pace for attending meetings or tribal gatherings. During my 21 years as an administrator of Indian education programs, I learned to wait approximately 20 to 30 minutes after the time that I had originally planned to begin parent committee meetings. I knew most of the parents would be late and when they

finally arrived would say, "I'm sorry for being late, but we were on 'Indian time.'" During our parent committee meetings we had several discussions on how parents could improve their being on time and teach their children to be on time for school and other social functions during the school year. And these discussions did make an enormous impact on many of the parents. We always saw a tremendous improvement in the attendance of Indian students and a lessening of their tardiness during the rest of the school year. Students' grades also began to improve and parents took a more active role in school activities. Very seldom would these parents or their children use the excuse of being on "Indian time."

We have to consider the role of education as a major factor in assisting Indian people in respecting time — the time allocated for meetings, the deadlines for completing documents, the due date for paying bills — or "Indian time" will continue to be used as an excuse for being late.

COMMENTATOR FLOYD BELLER is a retired Indian educator from the Ventura Unified School District in Ventura, California, and the WestEd Comprehensive School Assistance Program located in Oakland, California. He is of Chickasaw and Irish descent. He authored the *Title IX Indian Education Tool Kit* (2000, WestEd) and co-authored *The Directory of Indigenous Education Resources* (1998, WestEd).

Making Exceptions or Making Sense?

A Native American community does not adhere to the suggested model for community involvement in a project focused on saving groundwater nor do they meet deadlines for completing paperwork. The author of the case questions whether it is unreasonable to demand all participating communities to follow her agency's guidelines and wonders whether exceptions should be made for groups with different traditions. Issues of time and tradition are important to this case.

Process versus product — which is more valued?

For many people, at the heart of this case is the question of what the organization values. The grassroots, bottom-up structure of community activism has worked well in many sites and has led to measurable progress in saving groundwater. But, discussants wanted to know, what is more valued by the organization: the composition of the local groups or what they accomplish? This question leads to debates about the most effective ways for national organizations to work with local groups without sacrificing their own ways of doing business or ignoring local needs and customs.

How do you find a balance between accommodating and imposing cultural norms?

Some discussants attributed the author's belief that her organization's model for group composition must be followed and that deadlines must be met to her youth and desire to prove herself worthy of her new job. They speculated that with experience she would learn to allow for some "slack" in order for the project to succeed. Others agreed with her notion that exceptions should not be made for different groups. Inherent to this discussion is the maxim that "fair is not always equal." Also central to the discussion are disagreements over how a national organization can actually expect to control grassroots efforts by dictating the norms around which local people are expected to operate. The tension between compliance and volunteerism provides rich conversation among those whose work relies on soliciting the efforts of unpaid helpers.

Related to these general points concerning organizational norms is the specific context of the case and the clear misunderstanding of the role of the tribal elders. Those who have experience working in and with Native American groups have provided a different slant to the story that justifies the importance of an altered committee structure if the project is to be workable with the tribal community (see Floyd Beller's case commentary and Sharon Nelson-Barber's "A Comment on Culture"). Understanding each community in which one works is crucial to success, but how to go about learning the most important features of a culture's or community's norms? What type of research and planning should be undertaken in order to be able to effectively adapt to or negotiate with those with whom we must work? How do we decide which "rules" are fixed and which can be altered?

How do different ways that cultures view the environment affect program sustainability?

A tangential issue that arose in discussions of this case was the assumption that various cultures may actually view the environment and environmental problems from different perspectives. If this is true, how do we know what those perspectives are? And, then, how do/can those differences impact our programs? If the relationship of people to the environment is focused on the individual, can the same initiatives work as when the relationship is thought to be more communal? Again, how does diversity of audience or client affect the work one does?

Welcoming Diversity?

Ten years ago I was hired to develop a bilingual education program that would engage Latino students in environmental issues in ways that lessened their sense of alienation from school and fostered their self-esteem as individuals and members of the community. The Bilingual Environmental Education Program became very successful, offering field science and interactive learning activities about global environmental issues such as ocean pollution and deforestation that link the United States, Mexico, Central America, and South America. The program was available on a sliding-fee basis, to educate and empower school children, families, and adults. It opened a window of opportunity for thousands of Spanish-speaking children; during the program's first five years, over 14,000 students participated.

Three years ago, our parent organization shifted its focus from environmental education to promoting sustainable development in the Pacific Rim and neighboring countries. It also relocated out of our area. Without a sponsor, our program's agreement with the National Park Service to serve the local community would lapse and we would have to leave our beautiful park setting. Since the park was a wonderful learning resource, our parent organization helped us find another well-respected environmental group located in the same area that might be able to absorb our program.

Nature's Fund had worked primarily with white, upper middle income school groups. The fund operated on the sound business principle of remaining self-sustaining, largely through full tuition and fees; however, this meant that many culturally diverse and low-income school groups did not have access to the quality programs they offered. The previous year this organization had received a $1 million grant earmarked for a diversity initiative that would provide environmental education to a greater cross-section of the San Francisco Bay Area's student population, particularly those from underserved communities.

The match seemed almost perfect but the transition was not an easy process. From the start there were conflicting signals. On the one hand, the executive director seemed enthusiastic about this new collaboration. On the other hand, his board of directors, the education and outreach director, and the organization's president were not so sure this was the right move for them.

The negotiations seemed to drag on and on. Nature's Fund kept demanding more and more paperwork that seemed unrelated to the workings of the program. I began to wonder whether the organization was afraid of the unknown and uncomfortable being around people who looked different from them. I knew the board of directors and the fund's staff were concerned about my program's global focus and its emphasis on advocacy. Maybe they were also not really ready for the student population my program was serving.

When the executive director resigned six months after we initiated our first conversation, I thought that was the end of the negotiations. Without his support I didn't see how this transition was going to succeed. But I knew that in the highly diverse Bay Area this organization needed my program, and I wanted to help them provide environmental education to underserved school children. So many hours were spent trying to convince them that this program was really suitable for them.

After almost a year of negotiating, an agreement was reached and I became the first Latina (and the first non-white person) to hold a management position in the organization's 20-year history. Michael, a bilingual white male, came with me to help staff the program. Michael was committed to bringing environmental education to Latinos who because of language barriers would not ordinarily have access to the type of learning we offered.

Despite all the energy consumed by the lengthy negotiations, all the obstacles, and the probable bias, I was still excited about working for this well-respected organization. With their diversity initiative and extensive resources, I continued to feel that this was a perfect match. But I also knew coming to work here was going to be a challenging experience. Michael and I were given the smallest office in the building with a single desk and one phone line for the two of us. I brought in my own computer, chairs, table, and bookshelves.

After a few months, I noticed that many things were not as I expected them to be. Some of the staff were pleasant enough, but there were others who were openly hostile. I saw little or no interest in my program or in serving low-income children. The staff and administrators could not relate to them. They were more interested in the amount of money our program could generate than in the number of school children we could reach. For example, my supervisor wanted me to charge the same fee they were charging their regular school groups. When I explained that underserved kids could not pay that much, he answered that part of my and Michael's salaries had to be covered by those fees. He and other senior staff didn't understand why "those groups" couldn't pay their fees.

I soon found that my supervisor wanted to micromanage my job. He wanted to see every piece of work-related correspondence before I mailed it, and he wanted to sign it as well. He did that with no other director. I am a well-qualified professional. I have a teaching credential, a master's degree in education, and I am also bilingual in English and Spanish. I brought an educational background, knowledge, and teaching experience – not to mention a lot of experience and personal connections within the local community – that no one else in the organization had, not even the new executive director who, as the former outreach director, had taken a dim view of this collaboration from the start.

It seemed that the diversity initiative at Nature's Fund existed only in words, not in action. I am friendly by nature and used to come in saying good morning to everyone, but I soon felt that morning greetings must not be part of the organization's culture. The staff was very indifferent, very cold. I felt that they neither trusted me nor believed in my program's worth. I began to feel isolated, so the only person I felt comfortable communicating with was Michael. He was practically my only ally.

After working at Nature's Fund for about nine months, a major incident occurred that convinced me the match was not what I had hoped for. We often had problems with our computer and one day Michael called Alice, the program director who was also the tech support person, for help. I was in our office when she came in. Michael and I greeted her and thanked her for coming to help. She immediately asked, "What is the problem?" Michael explained the difficulty he was having. She leaned over, hit a few keys on the keyboard, and fixed the

I used to come in saying good morning to everyone but soon felt morning greetings must not be part of the organization's culture.

problem. Michael said to me in Spanish, "Rosa, qué tonto soy. Esto era una simple tontería" (Rosa, how dumb I am! This was something really easy to fix). I responded, "Qué pena haberla llamado para que viniera a reparar una simple tontería" (How embarrassing to have called her for something so simple to fix). Alice, who had previously mentioned that she knew some Spanish, reacted to our brief exchange by getting upset and began literally screaming at me. I was disrespectful, she said, how dare I speak in a language that she did not understand!

I was astounded, completely bewildered by her outburst. She knew that Michael occasionally spoke Spanish around the office, saying "Hola" or "Hasta mañana" to other employees. I knew there was nothing wrong with our speaking Spanish in my office, but I didn't want to have a confrontation with this person. Instead I immediately apologized to her. But nothing I said would placate this woman. Still furious, she declared that I was rude to her. It is interesting that even though it was my assistant, a white male, who initiated the Spanish conversation, she chose me to vent her rage on.

Concerned about the incident, I talked with the executive director. After I told him what occurred in my office, he said, "Yes, Alice talked to me already. You know she doesn't speak Spanish. She felt offended and disrespected by you. I think I understand how she felt. You should apologize to her." I answered that I already had. He repeated that I had to understand that Alice felt offended by me. His attitude was judgmental instead of objective. He didn't listen to me and I felt he was not supportive.

I left his office feeling devastated and frustrated. His lack of interest in resolving this unfortunate situation shocked me. I did not want to spend my time trying to make them accept me. The whole situation did not seem possible. I saw myself oppressed, alienated, and unfairly treated. I felt there was a lot of prejudice and racism in this "wonderful environmental organization" that had created an initiative purportedly "to embrace diversity." I went to my office and tears came to my eyes. I felt that I was the one who had been disrespected. I felt I could not continue working for this organization any longer. It was time to find another job.

Welcoming Diversity?

"Welcoming Diversity?" is written with a level of clarity and honesty about the world of diversity that engages the reader right from the beginning. The case starts by pointing out a current reality: the sense of alienation that lives in the hearts of many Latino students. Rosa, the environmental educator and author, recognizes that an environmental education (EE) program is a way to lessen that alienation. Working on environmental issues can move communities towards integration and unity and give individuals a sense of belonging. This social aspect of EE programs is not emphasized enough or used often as a strategy in working with culturally diverse communities. Yet the accomplishments of Rosa's program are evident in its ability to reach 14,000 students in only five years. This achievement affirms the type of success that an EE program with a social approach can have.

Rosa was aware that Nature's Fund "worked primarily with white, upper middle income school groups" and that her experience and program would greatly help the organization's diversity initiative. In the environmental education field, professionals who have never experienced diversity issues firsthand are too often placed in charge of developing solutions for those who have.

Initially it seemed to Rosa that Nature's Fund recognized her background and experience as an asset that could help them avoid a "colonialist" approach. But at the same time, Nature's Fund failed to recognize the inherent unfairness of limiting students' exposure to environmental education by their ability to pay.

Through her story, Rosa unveils deep cultural differences towards work. In Latin America, workers often do not have even the basic tools needed for their jobs, but here, in the United States, this is the exception more than the rule. When Rosa found herself in cramped quarters with few resources, she did not make an issue out of the situation. Instead she showed her willingness to support the organization and her allegiance and commitment to their common work. Could her colleagues have read that behavior as lack of assertiveness instead? Could this have added to their doubts about her work?

The differences in work "manners" are clearly described by Rosa. In Latin America, work is in a way an extension of family life. Greetings, hallway chats, and birthday celebrations are part of work "manners," whereas a greeting when you are busy in America can be considered an interruption or even rude. Unfortunately no one in Rosa's case showed understanding of these differences. As environmental educators we constantly encounter not only racial and cultural differences but also differences in perceptions about the environment that may or may not be related to cultural or racial issues. Acknowledging differences and the uneasiness they infuse into our professional work and relationships and keeping one's mind open may be a key step towards improving the environmental education field.

COMMENTATOR ISABEL CASTILLO specializes in developing participatory processes and strategies for environmental education programs. She founded and created the curriculum for Centro de Desarrollo Pequeño Sol, an elementary and middle school in Mexico. Ms. Castillo also developed a strategy to promote the creation of EE regional groups in Mexico and created guides and a process to adapt the *World Resources Institute Teacher's Guide* for use in Latin America. She is currently designing an EE strategy to help conserve agrobiodiversity and traditional agriculture in a Quechua indigenous community in Cotacachi, Ecuador.

Facilitation Notes

Welcoming Diversity?

A successful bilingual environmental education program loses its sponsoring agency and becomes affiliated with another large agency. The director of the program is the first non-white person to hold a management position within the new agency. Although the new agency has a recently funded diversity initiative, making this a "good match" in theory, the author does not feel that she or her program is welcomed or accepted. This case speaks to issues of cultural competency, clear communications, and respect. It asks what an organization should do to successfully assimilate new staff as well as prepare existing staff for working with those from differing cultural and ethnic groups.

How do group dynamics contribute to the problem described in the case?

Most people who discussed this case wanted to know three things: how much do individual personality and communication styles contribute to the problem; why was the staff so threatened by Rosa (was it her style, knowledge base, or clients she served); and what role does language have in creating tension? Though we can't find evidence for answering these questions, discussion about some of the more general issues proved interesting. Status and credentials affect group dynamics in general, and in this case it is fruitful to examine how self-perception may have impacted the interaction of those involved. Could the differences in cultures between Rosa and her new colleagues have been a contributing factor? Was it a matter of personal style, training, roles, or some combination that created disharmony?

How can a manager successfully integrate new members into a working group?

For a group to be able to function effectively and efficiently, members usually need to hold a common vision. How does that vision get created? In this case, discussants wondered whose vision it was that framed the work and whether it was shared. As we find ourselves in more and more collaborative working groups, we notice that different norms exist for each of these groups. It seemed clear that the Nature's Fund staff had a group norm prior to Rosa's addition to the organization. What could have been done to ease Rosa's introduction to the group? Should the stage have been set for discussions and agreements on ways of working together when Rosa was hired, and, if so, what might have been some strategies for doing that? Should the Executive Director have mediated and helped to establish better relationships once he was aware of the problem — and, again, what might be some strategies? Whose responsibility is it to train new members of a group in the already established group norms, or do the norms need to be changed when the group configuration is altered? Sharing the expectations and needs of each member of a group is also helpful when it may later be necessary for

diverse viewpoints to be integrated into a group decision; but when and how does this get accomplished so that no one is alienated?

What is the role of reflective practice for professional working groups?

As we get to know our colleagues better — both professionally and personally — our understanding of "where they are coming from" usually becomes clear and our ability to work together is enhanced. But how do we ensure that the groups we are part of continue to improve their working relationships and productivity? In this case, we do not know what (if anything) the Nature's Fund staff has done to grow as a group and learn from their practice. What kinds of activities could/should they have engaged in as a group to make sure that they continually refined their methods, increased their self-knowledge, and added to their knowledge of others different from them? How does a group plan for including formal debriefing and reflection activities as part of a way of working together, and then how does it go about making those sessions most productive?

Walking in someone else's shoes

Most of the discussion groups wanted to begin with a focus on roles, attitude, and actions/inactions from Rosa's point of view, but it is also important to look at the situation from the perspective of the Nature's Fund staff. Role-playing is often a particularly useful technique for highlighting different perspectives. In discussing this case, after identifying and discussing the key issues, five participants can be asked to respond to questions by playing the roles of Rosa, Michael, Alice, the Executive Director, and one other member of the staff, while several other participants can be asked to play the roles of outside consultants. Two separate scenarios can be created: in the first, the facilitator asks everyone to go back to when the initial decision was made to include the bilingual environmental education program within Nature's Fund. Rosa, Michael, Alice, the Executive Director, and the staff member should be asked about their expectations. The consultants then provide some guidance to the assembled parties about how to mold this new situation into a good working relationship that would benefit all — including the clients. In the second scenario, the parties are asked to put themselves at the point where the written case ends and to talk about next steps. This role-playing activity can prove to be enlightening, moving the discussion from "he should have, she should have" to a more general application of good practice. The conversation can then naturally shift to a discussion of what participants learned from this case that will impact their own work.

Sharon Nelson-Barber

A Comment on Culture

When I first agreed to comment on cases in environmental education, I was eager to respond to the variety of issues that I imagined might arise for environmental educators who work in diverse cultural communities. As a cross-cultural educator, I do not work directly in this field; however, my research in the Alaskan bush has positioned me to observe firsthand the practical intersection of environmental literacy and cultural diversity. In the harsh and remote context of rural Alaska, Yup'ik Eskimo villagers practice a subsistence lifestyle that is rooted in a profound respect for and spiritual connection with their ecosystem. Instruction about the environment begins at a young age and is typically hands-on. Youth are asked to closely observe their surroundings and to draw on prior knowledge to solve problems. Though there is an emphasis on correctness – because mistakes have survival consequences – there is sufficient time for private practice before proficiency is expected. Over time the process of observation, groupwork, and apprenticeship yields competent individuals who have mastered the requisite critical-thinking, decision-making, and problem-solving skills that will sustain them and ensure their longevity as a people – a truly authentic environmental education.

There are clear similarities between these time-honored approaches to teaching and learning and current research-based instructional techniques in which concepts are taught in meaningful contexts and students are encouraged to take responsibility for their learning (Trumbull, Nelson-Barber, & Mitchell, 2002). I imagined drawing parallels between subsistence communities' strategic use of local context and the successful approaches brought to light in the cases. However, as I began to digest the various dilemmas described by each author, I quickly saw that these issues had less to do with responsive pedagogy or recognizing the excellence that students might demonstrate in unique ways. They were all about the political, social, and cultural systems that encompass particular values and expectations about teaching and learning. And it was the sorting out of these kinds of distinctions that the authors of the casebook found most challenging.

An Insight Into "Biophobia"

One author's experience managing her East African students' "biophobia" made her keenly aware of "the different lens" that most of her students used when viewing the environment. An early enthusiasm to infuse hands-on environmental activities and concepts across her curriculum was soon tempered by students who were "conditioned to kill living things they found in their house or compound" because they were taught that "such things could harm them." Understanding that her students had been socialized to fear living creatures for practical reasons — we're talking "snakes, crocodiles, and hippos" — this teacher recalled her successes in previous classrooms where she used thematic units to engage students' experiential knowledge and to help reshape their thinking. Remembering the personal satisfaction she herself derived from physically interacting with chimpanzees at an animal orphanage where she volunteered, the teacher set about arranging a similar opportunity for her students, even fine-tuning personality matches between the children and the chimpanzees they would "adopt." Still, despite laying meticulous groundwork, which included weeks of preparatory study across the curriculum, the students did not care even to approach the animals when they met.

Of course the teacher comprehended this intellectually. Having worked in Africa for several years, she "sensed that many of the African students were still close to their traditional values and customs," and she understood, "in theory, at least," that this relationship to nature and certain learned behaviors helped "preserve people and their culture over time." However, for any teacher in the throes

of organizing such an effort — revisiting one's own learnings, arranging a site, developing a progression of lessons, and so forth — what can be missed is the steadfastness of the students' systems of belief.

We know from the literature that sociocultural background influences beliefs, values, knowledge, and experience (Luria, 1976; Rogoff, 2003; Solano-Flores & Nelson-Barber, 2001; Whorf, 1956). Collectively these influences impact a person's acquisition and expression of knowledge, which, for students, also surface in the styles of learning they bring to the classroom. Although this class was composed of "a mix of the urban privileged," who had a "pretty good grasp of English," many of the African students in the class spoke English as a second or third language. So in the midst of working to foster in her students "care and concern for the environment," the teacher was additionally needing to weigh their capabilities to understand and communicate their ideas. However, even when students are proficient in English, their sociocultural backgrounds still influence their behaviors and motives, which, in this case, materialized in the teacher's view as "biophobia."

It became clear that, despite her own enthusiasm for the activities, the teacher seemed to presume too much potential for common ground between herself and her students. Even though her students may have regularly experienced some blending of Western and traditional practices, taking in "new" understandings would not necessarily mean forsaking what they already believed. In rethinking what she had come to understand about her students' cultural knowledge, the teacher concluded that "interaction with a large, 'sexy,' endangered species" was hardly sufficient to reverse "the learning stemming from the socialization process."

What Contributes to "Toxic Disinterest"

The need to understand communities' underlying cultural knowledge is similarly the focus of "Toxic Disinterest?" — which includes an account of a local government's insensitivities to its diverse constituencies. First, after reading a newspaper editorial about the "irresponsible behavior" of local Hmong who were "eating fish caught in the...polluted harbor," the author, as the director of a multicultural center, was incredulous that warning signs posted around the harbor were printed only in English. Not only were snide remarks circulating in the community, but worse, when the author confronted an official from the agency responsible for managing the harbor, he was greeted with a cavalier attitude — "We put signs up.... Isn't that enough?" Implicit in such a remark is the assumption that anyone who cannot read English will find someone to translate, though the comment more likely suggests that everyone *ought* to speak and read English.

Though images of "melting pots" and "salad bowls" are continually summoned in celebration of our nation's diversity, there is lack of understanding about what honoring linguistic and cultural differences really means. The rhetoric of "English-only" initiatives and "Ebonics" controversies has led the general public to accept a narrow interpretation of what counts as "good" English, how language is learned, and, in general, how language works. Such misperceptions feed into fears that accommodating students with differing abilities means "watering down" education as a means to improve academic achievement. And most alarming, as the author discovered, the inaccurate and negative assumptions are intermixed with language and ethnicity and become insurmountable barriers to mutual understanding.

The fact is that locating opportunities to acquire the kinds of experiences that lead to an increased understanding of differing cultural perspectives is difficult. Reading about other cultures and visiting diverse settings is certainly a start. But there is no substitute for real, face-to-face, meaningful interaction with those you wish to learn about. In this case, the author was able to reflect on his own experiences working with the Hmong, which reminded him of a very important characteristic — their determination "to keep their original cultural ways alive."

Though these agrarian people have adroitly adapted to the urban environments in which most have found themselves after immigrating to the U.S., historically, no matter how oppressive the colonizer, they have absolutely rejected assimilation – something that Fadiman (1997) characterizes as the "stubborn strain in the Hmong character which for thousands of years has preferred death to surrender" (p. 51). Being faithful to Hmong cultural maxims means honoring particular practices, such as animism, but also adhering to specified norms of interaction organized within a traditional Hmong hierarchy. Fadiman (1997) further explains that this system dictates the social ranking of individuals (men above women, elders above youth) that includes responsibilities for problem-solving and decision-making. Although English and Hmong literacy levels are increasing among immigrants, the elder population, who also hold the most status, remain largely illiterate (Rai, 2003).

Imagine, then, that a younger person reads the "no fishing" signs. Fadiman (1997) suggests that correct protocol would dictate something like this: the youth would tell her mother, the mother her husband, the husband his elder brother, the elder brother the clan leader, and the clan leader higher level individuals, who would then communicate that an important message be sent to the community. So even though the posting of signs in the appropriate languages of the community should be an expectation, the real language issue here transcends the written word.

When a second water problem came to the author's attention later that year, he discovered even more "toxic disinterest." This time frequent beach closings and toxic waters had become a fact of life for a certain "long urban stretch populated by communities of color." And, for poor people, "a closed beach, where the water is free, robs them of an important asset." In an effort to engage community members and devise a plan for spreading awareness about the situation, the author surmised that others involved in environmental education and action would respond to the challenge. Surely such groups would embrace a plan to empower the community to handle its own issues. Perhaps not. One agency asserted they had "no money for a project like this." Another would "only get involved if there are policy issues at stake." Over time such encumbering excuses can daunt even the most dedicated individuals, leading them, like this author, to question whether their efforts are a waste of time. They journey from alarm to cynicism when they face the pervasive and far more menacing circumstances described in the next case.

Relationships Needed to Act Locally

After 13 years "working along the United States/Mexico border as a community organizer on environmental and health water issues," the author of "Act Locally?" understood the money crunch well. With social and environmental problems burgeoning on both sides of the border, her education team was immersed in learning "what it takes, both culturally and educationally" to build local competencies and "to help empower communities to bring about change." They had done the hard work of "forming deep relationships" with those they served, and although their funding had always been "hand-to-mouth," they thrived on their fine reputation and the earned respect of their constituents.

It is not hard to imagine the author's chagrin when she learned of the newly funded multimillion-dollar environmental monitoring program with "lots of big names behind it" that offered the "golden carrot of technology" to her schools, but little substance. The author was eager to discuss what her group had learned in their years of wrangling with issues of equity, local culture, and the environment. But with the new program "set," there was little need for this kind of input. What the new program needed was a letter of support because the RFP required minority participation. No bother, just a stamp of approval.

Is it likely that the noninclusive approaches evidenced in the cases "Biophobia?" "Toxic Disinterest?" and "Act Locally?" would actually deliver valid results? They certainly raise fundamental questions. For example, how do outsiders come to know constituents well enough to work with them effectively? And, more importantly, who ultimately makes decisions for the community? Will agencies understand the ways in which cultural settings inevitably interact with program goals and outcomes? How responsive will an intervention be to community values? In what ways will it engage knowledgeable community members in the enterprise?

The author of "Act Locally?" recognized that team effectiveness was associated with a willingness to extend into the community and acquire the level of understanding that can only come from direct, personal involvement. She had to wonder how the recipients of the new grant would go about establishing needed connections since their approach was to dominate — while the community demanded collaboration (see DeVos & Caudill, 1961; Greenfield & Cocking, 1994; Hofstede, 1983 for discussions of ways in which certain societies emphasize self-reliance and individual achievement while others promote group success). And what about the funder? Having recipients meet some kind of "demographic quota" is important in as much as the work needs to reach diverse communities. But shouldn't the RFP also insist that potential recipients demonstrate successful experience working in multicultural settings as a requirement for award consideration?

For anyone hoping to generate positive outcomes such as capacity building, issues of power need to be consciously addressed. In the case of the Hmong, simply inviting leaders to the table would not eliminate the power differential. Rather, bringing together individuals of different role types and backgrounds and involving them in work that "crosscut[s] the positions of participants" would likely "cultivate openness and sensitivity ... to the expressed and unexpressed concerns of different groups" (Weiss, 1998, p.106). The organization of those interactions may need to happen in a different manner for distinct groups, but the infusion of community perspectives needs to happen as the ideas are generated, not after the fact to validate a finished product or the imposed input of an outside entity (Dougherty, 1992).

Who Says What Is Culturally Neutral

The author of "Says Who?" would have appreciated having the opportunity to bring this kind of diverse representation to his table. In a stunning discovery, he encountered an ad campaign that used the figure Torquemada from the Spanish Inquisition — "a symbol of religious persecution, intimidation, humiliation, and physical torture" — to champion a state-run anti-litter campaign. Apparently the strategy was based on a "supposedly well-known skit" by the Monty Python troupe satirizing Torquemada's behavior. Still, given the highly multiethnic make-up of the local population, rather than presuming this to be a source of shared understanding, it was, at best, tasteless. At worst it was an indictment of Hispanic and Catholic communities and showed callous disregard for the "cultural communities that had been Torquemada's victims." Despite on-going criticism, the manager of the program believed that the "lighthearted treatment of the media spots would not be in bad taste" and folks would come to "understand the humorous context."

Though this assertion is indeed "insensitive," it more tellingly indicates how far outside the state official's range of cultural experience and/or knowledge the emotions inspired by this campaign fall. The author and the official are speaking from very different positions — from alternate cultural views — which, given the earlier discussion of belief systems and values, is a far more difficult communicative task than interactions among speakers who have a great deal in common and where much can be taken for granted in the interaction. When assumptions are not shared but instead must be created, more work is needed to achieve understanding. Background information must be provided, assumptions explained, objections anticipated with more use of specific examples and details. It is not surprising when people, like the author, enter into these discussions with the feeling, well founded in experience, that their perspectives are not likely to be taken seriously because the person they need to convince has already determined the appropriate response. Not only do individuals view the possibility of achieving real understanding a futile task — this author questioned whether his work was "more for show than for go" — they begin to second-guess even bringing up the hard issues because complaining may mean "appearing to be too much of an activist."

A Struggle Over Making Exceptions

The effects of not listening or granting legitimacy to differing perspectives has serious implications not only for the ways groups may contribute or cooperate, but also for our ability to discover more about what strategies work most effectively in these communities. This is the concern addressed by the next author, who wondered whether in her work with a tribal group she was "Making Exceptions or Making Sense?"

From the outset this new member of a groundwater protection project and one of her reservation community partners operated from very different vantage points. On the one hand, the American Indian community understood the importance of working to combat threats to their groundwater and showed great interest in the project. The project wanted to capitalize on this interest and actively sought community involvement to generate a grant proposal. On the other hand, community members were slow to agree, though they repeatedly suggested that the team "talk to the elders." The author followed through, devoting "countless hours" on the phone, and her boss met with the elders on site, to ensure that the community was on board and that their documentation was complete and prepared on time. Nonetheless, on deadline day, to her surprise, the tribe's application never arrived. Practically, this posed problems because, for one thing, the tribe would be out of sync with other partner groups. But the situation also led the author to question whether her team could "claim to be running a fair program if the standards for participation changed for each community."

Some of the answers can be found in contradictions that surface between the operational norms of the tribe and what the author believes them to be, which she expresses as follows:

>> "The tribe seemed determined to choose the very same top-down decision structure the program was designed to counteract."

>> The author was "stunned by the contrast between [the tribal team leader's] nonchalance and my palpable anxiety" about the delay in mailing in the tribe's application form.

>> "We wrestled with always changing our boundaries to accommodate this partnership."

The author's interpretations differ from the indigenous group's on several levels. Like the Hmong, most indigenous Americans adhere to prescribed leadership structures that defer to the wisdom of elders, who are not only respected for their knowledge and experience, but who also are accountable for the well-being of their communities. "Talking to the elders" is essential because the success of the work will often hinge on elder approval. Historically outsider interventions in Indian country have been largely intrusive and exploitative (Brown, 1971; Crazy Bull, 1997; Dougherty, 1992; Smith, 1999), so there often remains an underlying reluctance to speak freely to outsiders about issues that affect the tribe. In addition, there are strict rules about what knowledge is private, what can be shared, and who is entitled to speak about any of it. When elders in the community have not been consulted, informants may need to save face by appearing to answer questions through surface compliance, when in reality they can tell only part of the story because certain information cannot or should not be shared. The risk, of course, is that fragmented responses can be accepted as truths. The author's notion of counteracting the elder system of top-down decision-making would surely compromise the reliability and validity of the data.

Second, given that indigenous people favor community interdependence and often consensus, it is not surprising that now, as they exercise their sovereign right to control their own circumstances, they prefer to abide by their own maxims, such as taking the time for each community member's voice to be heard. Patience is highly valued even when this means a conflict with imposed deadlines. Aren't both the author and the tribe, then, wrestling with "boundaries to accommodate this partnership"?

Finally, the author's team came to understand that by bringing in a program designed to work for their usual audience — "the white, middle class of America" — they were also bringing in processes that were not tacitly shared by community members. The program's known methods that yielded good results in mainstream settings just did not work well on this reservation. As for the project's demands for certain paperwork and documentation, the author summarized it well when she remarked that the project and the tribe came to "the perhaps inevitable dissonance of requiring quantitative results from a community that considers itself inherently qualitative." In the end the project did strike a compromise and although the tribal team looked "different than the other community teams," that was okay.

Avoiding Cultural Paralysis

Those, like the "groundwater" tribe, who are always being asked to adapt, understand well the situatedness and limitations of different perspectives. The author of "Cultural Paralysis?" would have benefited from this kind of prior understanding as he sought ways to alter the tension that enveloped participants attending meetings organized to "address an environmental issue facing their diverse communities." In this case, a seemingly benign icebreaker activity designed for attendees to "get to know each other" triggered a chain of behaviors that ultimately disrupted the remaining sessions.

In response to the leader's request for participants to share something "unique" about themselves, two women, who identified as Native American, disagreed — in competition — it seemed, over who was "more native" or "would speak for the larger [native] community." The author was desperate to address the problem directly, but admitted "no understanding of the cultural 'rules' that were at play." The two women made it clear that this conflict was not going to be resolved by the author trying to "make things better." Nor were the participants who represented other racial and ethnic groups going to venture onto another group's conflicted turf.

The discord that arose here appears to relate to a number of assumptions taken for granted by each party. Teasing out the possibilities for the native women is of particular interest. First, although indigenous peoples share many common practices and values, they certainly remain distinct cultural and ethnic groups. Autonomy is highly valued and all groups have pride in their particular ways of knowing and being. So it is not surprising that the first speaker was "proud" to share her unique voice and perspective as a Native American. Still, not only to presume to "be the voice for the earth and native peoples," but also to articulate it publicly, is a clear breach of etiquette for many native groups. It is important to understand that these norms exist, but it also is important to recognize that such cultural expectations emerge in the structural features of discourse.

Though, as mentioned earlier, indigenous peoples' group focus and sense of interdependence has been well documented, they also value individual opinion. For example, examinations of indigenous elder oratories show that speakers are not expected to convince or persuade listeners to agree or accept their understanding of a topic. Rather the onus is on listeners to draw conclusions from the talk and take from it what is useful to them (Cooley & Lujan, 1982; Siler & Labadie-Wondergem, 1982). In sum, no speaker has the right to speak for another person. In many instances these stylistic elements extend to contemporary speech. But, in addition, norms surrounding who can actually speak for the group or represent the group perspective revert to local traditions of hierarchy, rank, and status within the community.

On another level, bragging about one's accomplishments or speaking about the future — essentially predicting one's success — is often considered bad luck (Bousseau & Toomalatai, 1993; Delpit, 1995; Scollon & Scollon, 1981). If the cultural expectation is that you would never promote yourself, "showing off" knowledge or experience or standing out in a situation is just plain rude. It is likely that the second speaker questioned how native the first could be after breaking so many rules with her opening sentence. At the same time, the author's well-intentioned effort to "empower" was turned on its head because, as he astutely concluded, the crux of the problem was "being afraid to treat a person of color as I would a white person." The native women were invited to the meeting "as equal participants," but somehow everyone else "made them more than equal and gave them control" they hadn't asked for.

Whose Time, Which Culture

Similarly to the facilitator in Cultural Paralysis?" perhaps the author of "Whose Time Are We Talking About?" anointed his students with unsolicited power, but in the guise of shared culture. Of indigenous descent, this environmental education specialist embraced the opportunity to design and implement a special program for native students at the national wildlife refuge where he worked. This was a "real opportunity to do something for the earth and Native Americans." It was a chance to honor culture by helping "young Native Americans develop or strengthen their relationship with the earth, a relationship sacred to their ancestors."

Still, despite the author's thorough efforts and planning, one particular behavior of the classes botched even the most meticulous preparation: their propensity to function on "Indian time," which essentially means "being late." The author observed that not only the classes, but, in general, Indian communities seemed to operate with little concern for the clock – events of all kinds seemed never to start on time. However, in a context in which classes are scheduled back-to-back and students from other communities tend to arrive on time, starting late can easily throw off the timing of the whole day. The added demands of constantly realigning plans within changing time frames led to great frustration for the author, who was left to conclude that this might be a "way that Native Americans rebel against highly structured society" or, being less conciliatory, maybe "just an excuse for being too lazy to be on time."

As a fellow Indian, the author understood the need "to respect the beliefs and traditions of each tribe." However, as a person socialized in the mainstream, he also understood the benefits of becoming competent in the style of the overculture, which facilitates choice-making and permits use of a common arena to share ideas and to educate others. How could he best bridge these understandings?

First it is important to consider the historical underpinnings of time as an organizer. Smith (1999) reminds us that beginning with colonization, the "belief that 'natives' did not value work or have a sense of time provided ideological justification for exclusionary practices which reached across such areas as education, land development, and employment" (p. 54). In fact, notions of "native people being lazy, indolent, [and] with low attention spans, is part of a colonial discourse that continues to this day" (pp. 53–54). And, as in earlier examples, many of these stereotypes are perpetuated through miscommunication.

The literature shows that when people misunderstand one another, they frequently make personal judgments and view the problems in attitudinal terms, often labeling the other person unfriendly, rude, or uncooperative (Feldstein, Alberti, & BenDebba, 1979; Gumperz, 1981). In Indian country, outsiders have been known to characterize the indigenous style of narration described earlier (one that is more circular than linear and gives responsibility to the listener) as rambling, unsure, or lacking confidence. When viewed in the context of appearing to care little about schedules, planning ahead, and so forth, indigenous speakers can be further perceived as indifferent or irresponsible (Gilliland & Reyhner, 1988).

If, however, we again consider the complex interconnection between language and culture and ways that culture and society shape an individual's thinking, it is telling that many indigenous languages have no word for time. Gilliland and Reyhner (1988) report that in these cases, most communication is in the present tense with some past tense forms and the future discerned from the context. Historically it is likely that "time" did not factor into the core ways of being and thinking in this community. What must be considered is that from then on, even when language shifts occur, the paralinguistic and extra-linguistic features of the heritage language will continue to carry over to contemporary speech [see also McCrum, Cran, & MacNeil's (1986) account of Gullah speech in South Carolina]. So even though the "late" classes and their teachers described here likely speak English as a first language, they would have been socialized to adhere to local ways of knowing and behaving.

Here, as in previous examples, the native classes and those from outside their community seem to be operating within different realities. And, as Luria (1976) contends, human thinking differs according to how social groups live out these realities. For the author of "Whose Time Are We Talking About?" time dominated. His reality was organized and scheduled by the clock. For the native classes, time was arbitrary and flexible. From their perspective, rather than focusing on the clock, it was more important to attend to immediate needs at home or elsewhere – to attend to human interaction in the moment (Bousseau & Toomalatai, 1993; Trumbull, Rothstein-Fisch, Greenfield, & Quiroz, 2001). One can certainly understand how confounding it can be when interactants operate from such different vantage points.

Though the author struggled to find the best solution, he was not willing to tacitly accept that "Indians are just laid-back and easygoing." He continued to seek answers. A positive next step would be to follow the advice of community members in the earlier case who specified "talk with the elders." So, in addition to approaching the teachers who need to get a handle on the situation, approach those responsible for the children themselves – the grandfather, the uncle, the auntie, the parents. Take advantage of the intricate system of extended family. Tell them what you need – the children on time. Explain why being late is disruptive, why it can be dangerous to hurry. Those responsible will respond when changing behavior contributes to community well-being. After all, as the author said himself, "I never heard that our ancestors ever practiced being late or that they were lazy."

Perhaps it will be through such an acquired lens that environmental educators, like all of the case authors, will learn more from indigenous groups and others who, like the Yup'ik, employ the critical skills needed to care for the environment. However, it is vital that all professionals directly confront the kinds of prejudices and biases earmarked in each of the cases. None is as palpable as in the final case, "Welcoming Diversity?"

Welcoming Diversity in Principle Only

In this instance a sponsorship change for the author's bilingual environmental education program rang a racist chord so jarring that it unearthed open hostility in the workplace. Following the relocation of her program's parent organization, a local "well-respected environmental group" with recently awarded diversity initiative monies seemed the perfect replacement. Early "conflicting signals" about taking on the program and the lengthy negotiations that ensued were troublesome, but not so unlike the challenges faced by other authors. Even being assigned to an inefficiently small office with no support is not uncommon for ancillary staff. However, as other elements began to creep in — a keen sense that her new sponsor had "little or no interest in [the] program or in serving low-income children" and a notable lack of sensitivity to the students' economic circumstances evidenced in queries about "why 'those groups' couldn't pay their fees" — the author became increasingly doubtful.

When her supervisor wanted to "micromanage" her job, this bilingual Latina professional with advanced degrees and established connections to the community she served was marginalized by behavior no other director encountered. Being asked to submit all of her written work for perusal and co-signature was humiliating. These expectations, combined with the now noticeable "cold" and "indifferent" daily interactions of her coworkers, added up to a working atmosphere of frustration, isolation, and disrespect. What irony, then, on a day when she and her own staff person publicly joked in Spanish about a computer glitch, that the author herself was accused by a monolingual coworker of being disrespectful. "How dare I speak in a language that she did not understand!" Interestingly, the other Spanish speaker was non-Latino, but no ire was directed toward him. Indeed, as the author concluded, the initiative of "this 'wonderful environmental organization,'" supposedly created "to embrace diversity," obviously "existed only in words, not in action."

Up to this point, it seems the author chose to put a more positive spin on her situation than the evidence could support. Rationalizing, she had chosen to interpret slights and signals of discord with tolerance. After all, it takes time for new entities to resonate with established ones. However, what now came to the fore was angry, deep-seated bigotry meshed and entangled with language. When there is little experience and understanding of other cultures and ethnicities, and these cultures and ethnicities are inextricably linked to their languages, one can understand why oral discourse often becomes the spark that elicits personal, negative, and frequently racist judgments [see also Baugh's (2000) discussion of linguistic devaluation and Smitherman's (1978) and Meier's (1998) accounts of misunderstandings about vernacular language use as evidence of cognitive disability].

In truth, the seemingly out of the blue "incident" described by the author aligns with what Steele (1990) terms an "objective correlative – an event that by association evokes a particular emotion or set of emotions" (p. 153). Steele recounts his own reaction after hearing a random person in an airport speak in a Southern accent as follows, "I could condemn this woman, or at least be willing to condemn her and even her region, not because of her racial beliefs, which I didn't know, but because her accent had suddenly made her accountable to my voluminous and vivid memory of a racist South" (1990, p. 150). Like Steele's, the monolingual coworker's reaction was likely an unconscious, visceral response to her own uncertainty, lack of understanding, and probable fear about things she knew little about – diverse people, diverse languages, diverse ways of being. These emotions were building up just as were the author's and,

given the highly unsupportive atmosphere, there were no opportunities or incentives to achieve common ground.

* * * * *

Though the stimulating examples presented in this casebook only graze the surface of complexities faced by environmental educators in diverse settings, they do delineate why these educators must judiciously develop discrete cultural competencies. One requirement is to learn as much as possible about partner communities, but equally important is the need to identify their own values and assumptions along with any predetermined judgments they might have. Because there is so much to learn from community members, it is essential that environmental educators have the skills to connect with them in meaningful ways. Doing so can deepen understanding of and respect for ideas, practices, and perspectives different from their own. Though no one comes to know "everything" about all people and all contexts, everyone needs to develop understandings about individuals, their settings, and issues apt to arise in those settings. Educators can then make better use of strategies that are consistent with those of community members.

All of these abilities lay groundwork for trust, which facilitates the kinds of connections that are needed to accurately share and interpret information and begin to learn about the realities of others. As illustrated in the cases, insiders and outsiders may have differing perspectives, but together they can accomplish mutual understanding.

Dr. Sharon Nelson-Barber, a sociolinguist, directs Culture and Language in Education at WestEd. This cross-program effort explores ways in which teachers more effectively teach the full spectrum of students in today's classrooms. Her work centers in particular on the teaching knowledge and abilities of educators in nontraditional settings and spans indigenous contexts in the lower 48 states, Alaska, and the Northern Pacific Islands of Micronesia. She also teaches at Stanford University's Center for Comparative Studies in Race and Ethnicity. She combines expertise in qualitative research and culturally competent assessment and evaluation with years of experience providing equity assistance to schools, organizations, and service agencies serving diverse communities, focusing in particular on cultural issues in the teaching and learning of mathematics and science. Dr. Nelson-Barber has been published extensively, is active in major organizations and meetings in anthropology and education, and serves on a number of national advisory boards and steering committees on teaching and learning in culturally diverse settings.

References

Baugh, J. (2000). *Beyond ebonics.* New York: Oxford University Press.

Bousseau, S., & Toomalatai, B. (1993). *Fa'a Samoa: Yesterday and today.* Los Angeles County Office of Education.

Brown, D. (1971). *Bury my heart at Wounded Knee.* New York: Holt, Rinehardt & Winston, Inc.

Cooley, R., & Lujan, P. (1982). A structural analysis of speeches by Native American students. In F. Barkin, E. Brandt, & J. Ornstein-Galacia (Eds.), *Bilingualism and language contact* (pp. 80–92). New York: Teachers College Press.

Crazy Bull, C. (1997). A Native conversation about research and scholarship. *Tribal College Journal, 9,* 17–23.

Delpit, L. (1995). *Other people's children.* New York: The New Press.

DeVos, G., & Caudill, W. (1961). Achievement, culture and personality: The case of the Japanese Americans. In Y. Cohen (Ed.), *Social structure and personality* (pp. 391–405). New York: Holt, Rinehart, & Winston.

Dougherty, M. (1992). *To steal a kingdom.* Waimanalo, HI: Island Style Press.

Fadiman, A. (1997). *The spirit catches you and you fall down.* New York: Farrar, Straus and Giroux.

Feldstein, S., Alberti, L., & BenDebba, M. (1979). Self-attributed personality characteristics and the pacing of conversational interaction. In A. Siegman & S. Feldstein (Eds.), *Of speech and time.* Hillsdale, NJ: Lawrence Erlbaum Associates.

Gilliland, H., & Reyhner, J. (1988). *Teaching the Native American.* Dubuque, IA: Kendall/Hunt Publishing Company.

Greenfield, P., & Cocking, R. (Eds.). (1994). *Cross-cultural roots of minority child development.* Hillsdale, NJ: Lawrence Erlbaum Associates.

Gumperz, J. (1981). Language, social knowledge and interpersonal relations. In M.W.S. De Silva (Ed.), *York papers in linguistics 9: Aspects of linguistic behaviour: Festschrift R.B. Le Page* (pp. 3–23). York, England: Department of Language and Linguistics, University of York.

Hofstede, G. (1983). National cultures revisited. *Behavior Science Revisited, 18,* 285–305.

Luria, A. (1976). *Cognitive development: Its cultural and social foundations.* Cambridge, MA: Harvard University Press.

McCrum, R., Cran, W., & MacNeil, R. (1986). *The story of English.* New York: Penguin Books.

Meier, T. (1998). Teaching teachers about Black communications. In T. Perry & L. Delpit (Eds.), *The real Ebonics debate* (pp. 117–125). Boston: Beacon Press.

Rai, K. (2003, November). Mandela assessment: The model, its cultural relevance and its application to Hmong refugee community-based agencies in Wisconsin. Paper presented at the annual meeting of the American Evaluation Association, Reno, Nevada.

Rogoff, B. (2003). *The cultural nature of human development.* Oxford: Oxford University Press.

Scollon, R., & Scollon, B. (1981). *Narrative, literacy and face in interethnic communication.* Norwood, NJ: Ablex Publishing Corporation.

Siler, I., & Labadie-Wondergem, D. (1982). Cultural factors in the organization of speeches by Native Americans. In F. Barkin, E. Brandt, & J. Ornstein-Galacia (Eds.), *Bilingualism and language contact* (pp. 93–100). New York: Teachers College Press.

Smith, L. (1999). *Decolonizing methodologies: Research and indigenous peoples.* London: Zed Books, Ltd.

Smitherman, G. (1978). *Talkin' and testifyin': The language of Black America.* Boston: Houghton Mifflin.

Solano-Flores, W., & Nelson-Barber, S. (2001). On the cultural validity of science assessments. *Journal of Research in Science Teaching, 38* (5), 553–573.

Steele, S. (1990). *The content of our character.* New York: St. Martin's Press.

Trumbull, E., Nelson-Barber, S., & Mitchell, J. (2002). Enhancing mathematics instruction for indigenous American students. In J. Hankes & G. Fast (Eds.), *Changing the faces of mathematics: Perspectives of indigenous people of North America.* Reston, VA: National Council of the Teachers of Mathematics.

Trumbull, E., Rothstein-Fisch, C., Greenfield, P., & Quiroz, B. (2001). *Bridging cultures between home and school.* Mahwah, NJ: Lawrence Erlbaum Associates.

Weiss, C. H. (1998). *Evaluation* (2nd ed.). Upper Saddle River, NJ: Prentice-Hall.

Whorf, B. (1956). *Language, thought, and reality.* New York: John Wiley & Sons, Inc.

GUIDE FOR THE
Facilitator

Guide for the Facilitator*

The more knowledgeable you are about the issues in a case, and the better you can anticipate the kinds of responses likely to emerge in a case discussion, the greater the odds that a rich exchange of ideas and learning will take place. Both the quality and the outcome of the discussion depend on what you as the facilitator do to prepare for it. In working with a group, why did you choose this particular case for this group, and what do you want to happen during the discussion? How will you introduce the case? What probing questions will you have in reserve if the conversation lags and needs to be reinvigorated? How will you close the session? These are just some of the things you must think through when preparing to facilitate a case discussion. To help you through this process, we are sharing what we have learned in the form of this guide.

Getting Started

Reading the case

You must have a good grasp of the case and its nuances if you hope to effectively facilitate its discussion. That means you will need to read the case several times — each time for a different purpose.

>> On your initial reading, what is your first impression? What excites you about the case? What bothers you? With whom do you relate? Additional readings may change your answers to these questions,

so it is important to write down these initial reactions and use them as a diagnostic tool. These empathic responses will help you gauge your values and later help you understand how participants react to the case.

>> As you read, ask yourself: What is this "a case of"? and What are the different ways to interpret this case? Note the descriptive words, key phrases, and dialogue used by the writer, especially early in the case as people or events are introduced. Each case has several layers of meaning, so each reading will yield more information and more understanding.

>> Reread the case with specific objectives in mind. Use one reading to identify the environmental education issues and another to look for issues of diversity — for example, how will the events in the case affect the author's ability to do his or her job? A third reading might focus on the author's role — what professional issues are at stake? The more perspectives you have on the case, the better you will be able to prompt broad-ranging discussion, thus reinforcing the idea that there is no single "right answer." With a range of perspectives in mind, you will be better

---

*With acknowledgement to *Facilitator's Guide to Groupwork in Diverse Classrooms*, edited by J. Shulman, R. Lotan, and J. Whitcomb (1998). New York: Teachers College Press; and *Dilemmas in Professional Development*, edited by T. Madfes and J. Shulman (2001). San Francisco: WestEd.

able to manage participation balance in the group should one person's viewpoint tend to dominate; your suggestion about another lens to look through can encourage the participation of others whose knowledge and experiences make them identify with the case in a very different way.

›› Look for pressure or stress points in the case, places where the author is confronted by angry coworkers, puzzled by a dilemma, or experiencing doubt about his or her actions. These serve as teachable moments in the discussion. You can prompt discussants to explore different interpretations of these events, helping them understand why the crises occurred. Such insights can help avert similar ordeals in their own work.

›› Look for subtle cues. Cases like "Welcoming Diversity?" can raise strong racial issues. But a real understanding of case dynamics requires examining the narrative in detail, perhaps making paragraph-by-paragraph notations. In many of the cases, information about people's racial, cultural, and gender perspectives is couched in subtle details. To discern this, you need to read between the lines, paying close attention to how the writer describes the socioeconomic, political, or historical features of people, organizations, or communities. Your goal is to continually try to elicit new cultural knowledge from the case that can help you and your groups get beyond "is this or is this not a racist encounter?" – a level of discussion that merely polarizes people. Instead, the group needs to look beneath the surface of what occurred.

Using the commentaries

The commentaries that follow each case can help you see the between-the-lines cultural indicators. Written by educators familiar with the context of the case, they are invaluable discussion aides when the group doesn't include a real cultural mix. These brief essays are meant to function as cultural informants, providing background that is meaningful and sometimes essential to discussion. Besides adding information, the commentaries can help you prompt discussants to question their own assumptions and understandings. Since people's perspectives are limited by what they already know, your role as a facilitator is to help them expand their ways of thinking by investigating the complexities that may be outside their own range of experiences. The commentaries can help you shape questions that move things in this direction.

A caution is needed here: The commentary on a case is not meant to signify the best way of interpreting the case. It serves as one of many lenses for interpretation and is offered to enrich the analysis by providing expert testimony or counterpoints to the ideas expressed through the case.

You might be wondering when and how to use the commentary. Should you have participants read the commentary at the same time as the case? Should the commentary be offered as another point of view after the discussion? Your decision depends upon the individual case and your purpose for using it. While reading the commentary after the discussion may preserve participants' original responses, reading it prior to discussion may broaden the issues participants are able to consider.

Using the facilitation notes

The facilitation notes accompanying each case are designed as a resource to help you plan the case discussion. These notes examine key issues that have arisen during actual case discussions and seek to provide an analytic interpretation that alerts you to potential problem spots. These notes are structured to help you analyze specific issues and they offer examples of probing questions, but they don't give you a specific way for moving a group through the case. Their purpose rather is to help you make your own plan for discussion, allowing for deviations as you gauge the group's direction. Anticipating that a discussion might take several paths, you can use the notes to identify discussion stages and plan probing questions that will enable participants to view the case through different lenses.

Planning the discussion space

People can be encouraged to fully participate in a discussion — or discouraged to do so — by the arrangement of the physical space in which the discussion is to take place. We have found that a U–shaped arrangement, with participants seated at tables on the outside of the U, works best. Settings like these allow participants to maintain eye contact with one another during a discussion and enable the facilitator to freely move within the circle. We usually ask participants to write their first names on the front of a folded sheet of paper to be placed on the table in front of them. We also place an easel with chart paper at the head of the U for recording major points made during the discussion. This allows participants to see how the discussion is progressing.

Planning the time

Peeling away the surface layers of a case and getting to underlying problems takes time. If you allow two hours for a case discussion, you should have adequate time to delve deeply into most cases. But what if you have only 90 minutes? This doesn't mean you shouldn't try to discuss a case, but it does mean you will have to plan your time accordingly. One suggestion is to distribute the case before the actual discussion and ask participants to read it carefully, jotting down questions and noting issues before the session. Because it's easy to get caught up in one section of the discussion and run out of time, it's even more important in a session of less than two hours to keep one eye on the clock. Stopping a discussion before you can bring it to closure is often more harmful than cutting short a particular section midway through the discussion.

Making your "lesson plan"

After you have a clear idea about what you want from a case (i.e., the purpose for using it, the issues to be examined, the plan it will lead to, etc.) and how much time you will have for the discussion, you will be able to write your lesson plan. Parceling out specific time slots for various segments of a discussion is very important to make sure you complete the discussion and allow participants ample time to reflect on the case and to share their personal experiences.

FIGURE 1. Structure of a Two-hour Case Discussion

Pre-discussion [20 min]
Introductions
Purpose and description of session
Ground rules for discussion
Read and notate the case

Part One: What's going on? [5 min]
What are the facts?

Part Two: Analysis [45 min]
Identify issues and questions
Analyze problems from multiple perspectives
Evaluate solutions proposed in the case

Part Three: Action/Principles of Practice [30 min]
Propose alternative solutions
Consider risks and consequences
Consider long-term vs. short-term options
Formulate generalizations about relevant good practice

Part Four: What is this "a case of"? [10 min]

Part Five: Reflection [10 min]
What did participants learn from this discussion?

It is also important for you to write out, in full, key questions you want to pose because the chances of remembering them while you are in the midst of the session are almost nil.

Figure 1 illustrates the major segments of a case discussion and how you might distribute the time in a two-hour session.

Although this structure appears linear, in reality discussions never proceed in a straight path. We do emphasize that it is crucial to thoroughly analyze the issues in the case, from various perspectives, before evaluating how the author handled the problems and before generating alternative strategies. In our experience, people are quick to make judgments and offer alternative solutions prior to adequately analyzing the situation.

Conducting the Session

Setting the stage

When beginning a new group, make it easy for participants to get acquainted with one another. Experience has shown us that allowing time for people to introduce themselves, or even using a simple icebreaker, sets a comfortable and warm climate and pays off later. If a group will meet several times, it is worthwhile to allow substantial time during the initial session for getting acquainted, establishing the rules and roles, and discussing the purpose for using cases.

Reviewing the agenda for the session (referring to a chart, transparency, or handout) gives participants an overview of not only what will happen but in what order. Take a few minutes to do this, both to minimize participants' frustration and to save time in the long run because the process becomes public. We suggest key statements be used, such as those in Figure 2.

Make sure that the ground rules are clearly understood prior to the discussion. Participants will need to overcome the notion that there is only one acceptable way to analyze each case. The purpose of the discussion is to foster an ethos of critical inquiry that will encourage multiple interpretations, conflicting opinions, and equal participation. Clear ground rules can help set the stage for this kind of discourse. Two major points should be emphasized:

›› Respect each person's contribution and point of view by listening carefully.

›› Do not interrupt! Wait for speakers to finish their statements before responding.

A third point to mention is that the discussion is not for the purpose of picking on the author but for understanding the issues and actions portrayed by the author.

›› Respect the author's openness in presenting the case.

Establishing the facts and generating questions

After the case has been read, an approach that works quite well in establishing a safe and comfortable way for people to engage with one another is to ask what information they have and to establish the pertinent facts in the case. Spend no more than five minutes to establish a shared understanding. This preliminary step allows you to check that everyone has read the same case (it happens!) and also allows you to stress the importance of differentiating between fact and interpretation. Sometimes participants become frustrated with this exercise; they want to jump right in to discuss the provocative issues. If this happens, you will have to judge how important it is to establish the facts before delving into larger issues. You can always refer

FIGURE 2. Sample Agenda to Post

Agenda
Welcome and introductions
Ground rules
Reviewing the case
Identifying the issues
Analyzing the issues
Alternative solutions
Principles of practice
What is this "a case of"?

participants back to the text if the facts of the case seem to be misunderstood or forgotten.

The next stage is to ask participants to work in pairs or trios to identify key issues and then convert them into questions about the case. We usually spend about 10 minutes total on this part of the process. You will have to tell the small groups that as compelling as the issues may be, they are not to discuss them or rush to try to solve the problems – there is a purpose to the process being used. After three to five minutes, instruct the groups to turn the issues they identified into questions. Using open questions, rather than statements, allows for meaningful discussion and multiple viewpoints. It is usually critical to provide a clear example of how to change an issue statement into an open question. You might provide Figure 3 as an example.

Once you have provided instructions for turning issues into open questions, visit the

FIGURE 3. Example of Turning an Issue Statement Into Open Questions

Issue	There are not enough instructors.	This is a declarative statement that does not provide any reason for discussion.
Question 1	Why doesn't the refuge have more instructors?	The case may not provide any information for answering this question. Not very useful.
Question 2	What is an appropriate instructor/ class ratio at the refuge?	This question, situated in the case itself, prompts discussion.
Question 3	What is an appropriate instructor/ class ratio for outdoor interpretive activities?	This question allows for discussion and can lead to establishing principles of practice because it is situated in a more generalized context.

groups and redirect any that have not understood the directions. When groups have generated several questions each, record on chart paper one question from each group. Continue collecting questions, one at a time per group, until all points are presented. This process serves to engage all members of the group immediately. It also provides a list to refer to during the discussion and to use to make sure that all points are addressed. The list also provides you and the group with a preview of the range of interpretations within the group, before the discussion begins. The list makes clear that there are many ways to look at a case, and it should help to prevent the discussion from becoming fixed on a particular view.

After completing the list of issues stated as questions, ask the group to decide where they wish to start the discussion. Discussants report that this gesture is important. It sends

a subtle message that you respect the group's agenda and that you won't impose your own. It also empowers some participants who might otherwise remain silent to speak up. If the decision-making process seems unmanageable, one effective technique is to give each person four votes to distribute in a variety of ways to rank their preferred focus for discussion of the issues. As you cycle through the issues, ask people to use their fingers to indicate how many of their votes they wish to cast for each issue. Or you can distribute sticky-dots and have people place them next to the issues they want to discuss.

For groups that know you and each other well, you might begin more directly, providing a focus question for immediately examining a key issue. If you decide to do this, be sure you consider your opening question carefully because it will set the tone for the entire discussion. The advantage of this approach is that it usually starts the discussion off in a lively way. The tradeoffs are that some participants may feel inhibited about bringing up their own issues or may feel that you have a fixed agenda for the discussion.

Facilitating the discussion

Once the initial focus of the discussion is established, we suggest the following:

Analysis. Analyze the issue(s) from the perspectives of the different actors in the case. Adequate analysis often takes at least half the discussion.

Evaluation. Examine the author's strategies for handling the problem(s).

Alternative solutions. Generate strategies for handling the problem(s), making sure to consider the risks, benefits, and long-term consequences of each strategy.

Principles of practice. Formulate some generalizations about good practice based on this and any prior case discussions, participants' experiences, and their theoretical understanding.

What is this "a case of"? Moving up the level of abstraction, link this case to more general categories; rich cases are by nature "of" many things.

In a typical discussion, initial focus is on the specifics of the case and an analysis of what happened. In the diagnosis of what went wrong, comments often reflect participants' personal experiences and theoretical understandings. The effectiveness of the analysis depends upon your repertoire of questioning techniques and how they encourage reflection. Different types of questions (e.g., open-ended, diagnostic, challenging, predictive, and hypothetical) serve different purposes. The facilitation notes accompanying the cases contain examples of types of questions. You should be prepared to follow participants' responses with probing questions that deepen their reflection. When participants begin to ask questions of one another, rather than continually orienting their remarks toward you, this is a positive sign.

Trouble spots

Each case discussion is different and takes on a life of its own. This uniqueness offers a great challenge to the facilitator. At times discussions may seem to be at an impasse, or it may seem that participants are ignoring information you feel is key to understanding the case. At such times, you may need to shift the topic. One way to do this is to say that you've spent a lot of time discussing a particular topic, then ask about viewing it from another perspective. Another tactic is to play devil's advocate and to introduce the missing component as a counterpoint.

Occasionally it may be necessary to push ahead by summarizing the key points of the discussion so far or offering additional information for people to consider that could help move the discussion along. Often a facilitator has useful background information, such as a law or regulation or some research that may be pertinent to the discussion. Another strategy that can offer a welcome change of pace is to incorporate activities such as small group discussion or role-playing (e.g., see the facilitation notes for "Welcoming Diversity?" for an example of this strategy).

Be sensitive to the possibility that there may be tension between your agenda for the discussion and the group's agenda. This requires a delicate balance. If you stick to your plan without letting the participants move in the direction they prefer, you communicate that you are in control and they may hesitate to contribute their issues and concerns. If you allow the participants to control the agenda, you abrogate your role as a leader. One way to get around this dilemma is to look for opportunities to build on participants' ideas rather than offering your own. Another is to remind them that as facilitator you will challenge their ideas and push them to defend their views, regardless of their position. Ultimately you are trying to move participants from reflection to problem solving and a willingness to investigate their own practices.

Closing the case

Another major challenge is helping participants synthesize and reflect on what they learned through the discussion. Participants should have the opportunity to identify new understandings as well as unresolved conflicts and questions before the discussion concludes.

One approach is to ask participants to reflect on the case and respond to the question What is this "a case of"? It asks participants to characterize a particular case in relation to other cases, to their own experience, and to the conceptual categories with which they are familiar. In our experience, this technique has been extremely valuable in helping participants move away from the particularities of a specific case and begin to identify the variety of categories the case represents.

Another way to bring the discussion to closure is to ask the group to spend a few minutes doing a "freewrite," responding to such questions as What did you learn from this case discussion? Do you have lingering questions? What part of the discussion did you find most challenging? How can you relate what we discussed to your own experience? Many people appreciate the opportunity to synthesize their thoughts in writing prior to sharing them with the larger group.

Role of the Facilitator

Although you may have more background than the group you are working with, as a facilitator you should not assume the role of expert during a case discussion. Your responsibility is to elicit alternative perspectives and help participants analyze them. Your role is that of active listener, and you should reflect this through your words and body language, so that participants know that you have heard, understood, and accepted what has been said. You will also need to have a set of probing questions available to help clarify and challenge assumptions and proposed strategies that participants raise during the discussion.

If people seem to be quick to accept — or reject — ideas before reflecting on different perspectives, you may offer other slants for consideration. Your goal, however, is not to lead them to a particular point of view or conclusion, but to help them come to their own conclusion about the best course of action. Perhaps one of the most difficult aspects of leading a discussion is the possibility that participants may leave with what appears to you to be the wrong point of view. You may feel compelled to give them the "correct answer" or feel impatient when they struggle to reach a conclusion. Be patient. It takes time to change beliefs, and being told what to think is rarely effective.

Your job is to do the following:

›› Maintain a nonjudgmental stance.

›› Probe and challenge assumptions.

›› Synthesize, paraphrase, and clarify disagreements.

›› Ensure equal and full participation; keep track of those who want to speak.

›› Encourage quiet members to contribute.

The facilitator's challenge is to build an ample world of ideas for the group to explore, then to move the discussion up and down a ladder of exploration: up to higher principles, back down to very discrete practices, then up again – in other words, to repeatedly move from the level of an opinion swap to the desired level of applied knowledge. How do you do this?

Try not to become emotionally involved in what is being said. If you keep some distance and continuously analyze how the discussion is going, you will be more effective. Pay attention to equitable participation.

Periodically tie up loose ends, summarize what has been established, and move along to the next step. This will keep people from repeatedly coming back to the same points and digressing so far that the case ceases to be the focus.

After there has been an evaluation of how the author dealt with a particular problem, ask what alternative strategies could have been used and analyze the risks and benefits of each. Such questions can inspire people to make judicious changes in their own situations.

When appropriate, ask participants to come up with generalizations or principles based on this and other case discussions. This step will help to develop participants' capacity to transfer what they learn from the analysis of a particular case to similar situations they may encounter in their own work.

Remember that you are teaching the skills of case analysis. Ultimately, you are moving participants toward applying what they are learning to their own behaviors, but only in-depth analysis will allow that learning to occur, and the required skills take time to develop.

Then, after you have conducted the discussion, reflect upon what transpired. Think about both the process and the outcomes. Make notes for yourself, so that the next time you facilitate a case discussion you can benefit from your own learning.

If you have comments about the cases or the facilitation notes, or want to share with us what you have learned from the use of the cases, please write to us at *tmadfes@wested.org*. We hope that this book will provide you and your groups with tools for rewarding group discussion and interaction. The result can be a powerful experience in professional development.

Please note: You may reproduce up to 30 copies of a single case for use in your work. Permission is not granted for any other reproduction or dissemination.

Case Author Biographies

Brady Beecham

Brady Beecham's education in water began at the Groundwater Foundation and will be a lifelong passion. Currently, she is working on water and public health issues at the Nebraska Department of Health and Human Services in her hometown of Lincoln. She is always looking for new cultural perspectives on water and will spend next year as a Rotary Scholar on the Ganges River in India. After that she plans to attend medical school.

Hilda Castillo

Hilda Castillo's professional experiences include more than 15 years in teaching as well as work in planning, development, implementation, and coordination of education programs in her native Venezuela, in other Latin American countries, and in the U.S. Ms. Castillo holds a master's degree in education from Sonoma State University, where she also worked as academic coordinator/associate director for the Upward Bound program and PreCollege Programs.

Elaine Jane Cole

Elaine Jane Cole is currently the project manager for the Oregon Collaborative for Excellence in the Preparation of Teachers. In her spare time she is a Ph.D. candidate at Antioch University studying leadership and education for environmental sustainability. Previously she worked at Portland State University as a science resource specialist.

Joe Heimlich

Joe E. Heimlich is a senior research associate with the Institute for Learning Innovation in Annapolis, Maryland. He is also a professor of environmental education and interpretation at the Ohio State University, School of Natural Resources. For more than 20 years he has been working in the OSU Extension in community development dealing with environmental issues in communities. He has served on the board and as president of North American Association for Environmental Education.

Hyder Hope Houston

Hyder Hope Houston, president and CEO of Diversity in Environmental Education, has over 25 years of experience in community education, outreach, and organization. She was recognized nationally as a Groundwater Hero during the 25th anniversary celebration of the Safe Drinking Water Act. Currently she serves on the National Review Board of the Groundwater Foundation. She is a past member of the National Environmental Education Advisory Council, U.S. Environmental Protection Agency.

J. Allen Johnson

J. Allen Johnson is a graduate of Valparaiso University School of Law (Law Review). He is licensed to practice in the District of Columbia and the state of Indiana with a specialty in litigation. He is also a stage director and university administrator. Currently he serves as the executive assistant to the chancellor at Purdue University, Calumet.

Lisa LaRocque

Lisa LaRocque is the founder and codirector of Project del Rio, a binational environmental education program in the Rio Grande watershed. Lisa also provides training in real-world investigations for many school districts, facilitates diversity outreach programs nationally, and develops sustainable development curriculum.

Tania Madfes

Tania Madfes, Ed.D, is a senior research associate at WestEd, where she directs both professional development and evaluation projects related to mathematics and science education. She was editor of *Dilemmas in Professional Development: A Case-based Approach to Improving Practice* (2000, WestEd) and lead author of *Learning from Assessment: Tools for Examining Assessment through Standards* (1999, WestEd/NCTM).

DouGlas Palenshus

DouGlas Palenshus's own multicultural heritage and artistic background have provided a broadly balanced perspective on inter-cultural community relations. He is the outreach coordinator for the Water Quality Program at the Washington State Department of Ecology. He has been involved with environmental work since 1977 and has a master's degree in environmental science.

Nick Plata

Nick Plata works as an environmental education specialist at the Wichita Mountains National Wildlife Refuge. He is a member of the Comanche Tribe and the great-great-grandson of Comanche Chief Tabananika. He graduated from Cameron University, where he majored in biology with a minor in chemistry.

Dawn Wrench

Dawn Wrench is the director of the Student Environmental Congress, a program of Earth Day Coalition in Cleveland, Ohio. She helps students and teachers connect with their local environment while equipping them to make a difference in the quality of their neighborhoods. Previously, she was an educator at various environmental education centers and camps.test

North American Association for Environmental Education

The North American Association for Environmental Education (NAAEE) is a network of professionals and students working throughout North America and around the world to promote a healthy and sustainable environment through education. NAAEE is committed to developing the partnerships and policies needed to increase cultural diversity in environmental education (EE) leadership and programs.

NAAEE provides support for environmental educators and other educators through a variety of programs and activities. Since 1971, NAAEE has provided the field's premier annual international conference, developed programs to serve environmental education professionals and stakeholders, and published resources for EE practitioners and researchers. NAAEE activities include the following:

- Supporting EE Capacity Building. NAAEE, through its state Affiliate Partnership, offers professional development at the NAAEE annual conference and follow-up support to help build the understanding and skills needed to create comprehensive and sustainable EE programs at the state level.

- Excellence in Environmental Education. NAAEE promotes use of the Guidelines for Excellence in Environmental Education created by the National Project for Excellence in Environmental Education. The guidelines are used to develop and screen EE materials, create K–12 instructional programs, and prepare educators to include EE in their teaching.

- Electronic Access to EE. NAAEE's EE-Link (http://www.eelink.net) provides environmental educators with online access to information about EE training, programs, jobs, events, organizations, resource reviews, and consulting services on Web-based EE information management. NAAEE's organization website (http://www. naaee.org) offers many benefits to members and other EE professionals.

- Mainstreaming Environmental Education. NAAEE is developing EE program standards for the preparation of teachers in collaboration with the National Council for the Accreditation of Teacher Education (NCATE). NAAEE is also working with its state network to develop state and national certification in environmental education programs for nonformal educators.

For more information about NAAEE, please visit http://www.naaee.org or contact us at 2000 P Street, NW, Suite 540, Washington, DC 20036.

Environmental Education and Training Partnership

The Environmental Education and Training Partnership (EETAP) fosters environmental literacy in America's schools, nature centers, government agencies, and other institutions. It does this by identifying and implementing essential professional development and support services for educators working in formal and nonformal education settings. EETAP is committed to ensuring that ethnically diverse and low-income communities benefit from and actively participate in education that advances student learning and environmental literacy.

As a consortium of leading national environmental education organizations, EETAP

- has developed national guidelines for environmental education,
- is helping to build the understanding and skills needed to create comprehensive and sustainable environmental education programs at the state level,
- delivers professional development workshops in environmental education,
- offers an online environmental education course and resources,
- collaborates with national education associations to promote the value of environmental education as an effective teaching approach for advancing student learning and environmental literacy, and
- develops and distributes a variety of resource materials to education professionals.

These activities help increase public knowledge about environmental issues and enhance the critical thinking skills necessary for individuals and their communities to make responsible environmental decisions.

The U.S. Environmental Protection Agency's Office of Environmental Education supports EETAP through a cooperative agreement with the University of Wisconsin-Stevens Point, where the project is based at the College of Natural Resources. For additional information about EETAP and its partners, please visit http://www.eetap.org.